Beyond the Shadow of Doubt

Dr. Mark J. Chironna

BEYOND THE SHADOW OF DOUBT by Dr. Mark Chironna
Published by Creation House
A part of Strang Communications Company
600 Rinehart Road
Lake Mary, Florida 32746
www.creationhouse.com

Unless otherwise noted, all Scripture quotations are from the
New American Standard Bible. Copyright © 1960, 1962, 1963,
1968, 1971, 1972, 1973, 1975, 1977 by the Lockman
Foundation.
Used by permission. (www.Lockman.org)

Scripture quotations marked KJV are from the
King James Version of the Bible.

Scripture quotations marked PHILLIPS are from
The New Testament in Modern English, revised edition.
Copyright © 1958, 1959, 1960, 1972 by J. B. Phillips,
Macmillan Publishing Co. Used by permission.

Scripture quotations marked THE MESSAGE are from
The Message, copyright 1993, 1994, 1995.
Used by permission of NavPress Publishing Group.

Library of Congress Catalog Card Number: 00-110749
International Standard Book Number: 0-88419-731-X

1 2 3 4 5 6 7 8 VERSA 8 7 6 5 4 3 2 1
Printed in the United States of America

Dedication

This book is dedicated to all those who have
known the struggle of having great doubts mingled
with their great dreams.

Acknowledgments

I want to thank a number of people for their help and assistance in bringing this project to completion:

- I want to thank the team at Creation House and Stephen Strang for their belief in my call to write.
- I want to especially thank Rick Nash who wouldn't let me give up on the project and held me to the conviction that it was a book that needed to be written.
- I want to thank Peg de Alminana for reminding me again and again to write in such a way that the reader will be able to connect and for her patience with my many changes until I got it to where it needed to be.
- I want to thank Cheri Ingram for teaching me about the importance of always giving a prescription for any point I make so that it sticks in people's hearts and minds.
- I want to thank Terry Clifton for his ongoing support and assistance, his ideas about the flow and layout of the book graphically, the wonderful sounding board he is to me and his tireless zeal to enhance all the things I have been assigned to complete.
- My thanks also to Leonard Sweet for befriending me and for the way he has stretched my sense of applied imagination as it relates to the postmodern world we are entering in this new millennium and the need for us to be relevant there.
- Finally, I want to thank my wife for putting up with me again during the seasons (day and night) of writing and rewriting.
- I want to thank my two boys who make it worth it all because of their ability to teach me how to see the world again through young and new eyes, even in choppy waters.

contents

I know nothing, except what everyone knows—

if there when Grace dances, I should dance.

—W. H. AUDEN, POET

Foreword

Dance the Night Away
by Leonard Sweet

One of the landmark spots in
New York City is called the
Rainbow Room. At the top of the GE

One of the landmark spots in New York City is called the Rainbow Room. At the top of the GE building at Rockefeller Center, it is famous for two things: a panoramic view of the city from its 64th floor, and a place where you can dance the night away.

The Rainbow Room is another name for the kingdom of God—a place where you can dance the night away—the night of despair, the night of disease, the night of depression, the night of doubt, the night of death. "The people that walked in darkness have seen a great light. On those who live in a land of deep shadow a light has shown." (See Isaiah 9:2.)

Dance the shadows away. Our beings are designed to dance night viii

into day, sadness into gladness, doubt into faith. Super-string physi-
cists now define matter as "dancing filaments of energy." Even the
"turning dance" of Planet Earth spins the night into the sunrise of
surprise and hope. "The whole creation is on tiptoe," Paul antici-
pates the poet Denise Levertov here, "to see the wonderful sight"
(Rom. 8:19, PHILLIPS). No wonder many poets and philosophers
liken the life of faith to "a kind of dance."[1] Not to mention Jesus.

Joy is a spiritual obligation. Robert G. Tuttle, Jr. likes to tell his
students that "if you can't have more fun doing God's thing than
the world can doing its own thing, then you should give your faith
another look. Something is missing."[2] Doubt and despair are not
victimless "crimes" of the spirit.

Why then are so many people's spiritual lives stuck on ground
floors or locked in basements, afraid of elevators that lift life to the
Rainbow Room heights? Why do so many of us not "feel right"?
We know something's wrong. We don't feel comfortable in our
skin. The tingle of tiptop, tiptoe living is at best a far-off memory.

Our escalating problem is caricatured by two persons. One is
perched on the top of a solid steel flagpole. A weightlifter slams
the bottom of the pole with a large sledgehammer. What happens?
The vibrations travel quickly through the solid steel up the pole.
Almost the full force of the hammer blow has been transferred to
the top of the pole, as man and pole rock and roll.

Now imagine the same person sitting on top of a mountain of
fat. The same muscleman strikes the bottom of the mountain of fat
with the same sledgehammer. Instead of BOING!, it's KERPFLOP! The
fat absorbs the blows, transferring none of the hammer's original
clout to the man at the top of the mountain of fat.

Many of us are sitting on mountains of fat. The BOING! of life
can't reach us because of all the superfluity in our pot-bellied, pot-
boiler lives. We spray down problems with a money hose as our
souls get more fat and fatuous. As our breakthroughs are mostly

dead-ends, we hear the distant rumbles of BOING! amid slight tremors. We know *The World Is Not Enough*, as the James Bond film puts it, and our hunger for the spiritual is palpable.

> Never trust a spiritual healer unless he knows how to dance.
> —OLD ASIAN PROVERB

In *Beyond the Shadow of Doubt*, Dr. Mark Chironna shows us how to rid ourselves of life's excess and extraneous so that our souls can sway and swing and dance again.

I invite you to read this book in the same way the ancient rabbi sent his disciple to learn from a fellow rabbi. When asked what he should learn, what parts of the Torah, the teacher answered: "I am sending you to learn from him—not words of the Torah, but how he ties his shoelaces!"[3] It's Chironna's mentoring in the small daily things, the details of walking through the valley of our shadows, that shows us how to turn every "though" into a "through" ("*though* I walk *through* the valley of the shadow") by the addition of one little letter.

"It ought to be a commonplace," Cambridge professor John Oman used to say, "that the foundation of a good life is a good habit." Habits of the holy enable our hands and our fingers and our feet to remember. The memory of the body is in some ways more important than the memory of the mind. For what happens when the mind is in turmoil and forgets? The body remembers.

One of the great architectural sites in Florence, Italy is the Foundling Hospital, built in 1419. Tourists from around the world pay homage to the arcade, designed by Filippo Brunelleschi, which became the ideal of excellence for Renaissance architecture.

What most people forget, however, is the purpose of this building. When mothers were unable to care properly for their infants, they brought them to the entry door, placed them on the *rota* (a circular tray that swiveled from outside to inside) and rang the small bell by the door. From inside a nurse turned the wheel that rotated the *rota*, and the baby vanished into the care of the church's healing community.

The building today houses pediatric clinics, children's and family services and a museum that features an extraordinary art collection. Inside one glass display case are some of the artifacts from six hundred years of turning that *rota*—blankets, buttons, ribbons and medals...many of them cut in half. It seems that mothers would keep half of what they left with the baby in hopes that some day their fortunes would change, life's clouds lift and the shadows flee away. Then they could reclaim their child from the care of the church.[4]

Life sometimes goes into reverse. The clouds of glory dissolve into feet of clay. When it does, whatever is most cherished in your life, you can bring it to God in trust and confidence, and leave it there. Chironna shows you how.

- When your heart is worn out with worry, trust in God for a new heart.
- When the body is willing, but the brain isn't, keep the Rainbow Room clean and maintained.
- When the music of faith stops playing in your life, let God lead the dance.
- When you can no longer dance even with God as your dance partner, let the church dance for you.
- Then when your mind is healed and your faith secure, you can pick up the pieces, pick up where you left off . . . and dance.

Here's a book to help us dance the night away.

Section I

Blocks to Faith

Beyond
the
Shadow
of
Doubt

To confront a person with his own shadow is to show him his own light.

To confront a person with his own shadow is to show him his own light.

—CARL JUNG

Chapter 1

Drowning in an Ocean of Doubt

Henry often displayed a restlessness that appeared to keep his internal motor running at high speeds even when he was in neutral gear. We were on our way to a seminar I was conducting and were sitting in slow-moving traffic on Interstate 79 in West Virginia due to heavy sleet and snow. The road was beginning to ice up, it was nearing nightfall, and as Robert Frost might have said, we had "miles to go before we sleep."

Henry had been behind the wheel for a number of hours through the winding passes and steep inclines of the mountainous terrain, and now we were inching along with traffic slowed to a snail's pace. The world was not moving fast enough for Henry. It wasn't paying enough attention to him either.

Every move that Henry made appeared to be tied to a need to be seen and approved of by those whose acceptance he seemed to value. He demanded acceptance—albeit unconsciously—from those he perceived to be in authority. He also had to be in charge of others who did not fit his description of the authority he valued, no matter what. His need to take control and take charge all the time, expecting that the world would move out of his way, seemed to belie a deep-seated insecurity. Once Henry was in the driver's seat, his hidden "drivenness" would show up unmasked.

His willingness to serve with an eager spirit seemed exemplary, but often it was clouded by needs-driven behaviors, approval seeking and a need for continual validation that had become deeply anchored within his soul. If anyone suggested that he was crossing boundaries that were not acceptable, outwardly he would seem apologetic. But inwardly he could not accept it as reality. The behaviors that drove him to cross boundaries and take on assignments that were not his continued again and again.

As Henry grumbled about the drivers who were keeping him from speeding up, I offered to drive, as I was not excited about hydroplaning on sleet and ice.

Henry pulled over, and we changed places. I gradually pulled back into traffic as a slow-moving tanker truck passed us. The slick road forced traffic into only one lane, and we fought the salty splatters on our windshield as we inched along. When it seemed an appropriate moment in the conversation, I decided to ask Henry a question. As best as I can recall, the conversation went something like this:

"Henry, do you feel driven to prove your worth?"

"Oh yeah!"

"Any idea why you feel that way?"

"Probably because of my background."

"What about your background?"

"Well, you know, I was raised in New York in a tough neighborhood, and my dad was really strict. He never expressed love or affection."

"What was it like growing up?"

"My brothers and I grew up tough. We learned how to survive."

"Did you get along?"

"For the most part, although I had some struggles with one of my brothers and with my dad."

"Would you feel comfortable explaining that to me?"

"Sure. Did I ever tell you I was diagnosed with epilepsy when I was a kid?"

"Really? No, I never knew that!"

"I remember making weekly trips to the hospital where they put these wires and things on my head."

"Sounds like the electrodes and pins they used on me when I had a brain wave scan."

"Yeah. Well, I had to go often, and then, suddenly, the doctors said I outgrew the epilepsy."

"So, there's no trace of it left in your life?"

"No, it went away."

"How did you feel when it went away?"

"For the most part I still always felt like I missed something growing up."

"Is that why you feel that you have to constantly drive yourself so hard to feel that you are important?"

"Oh, yeah!"

"May I ask you another question?"

"Sure!"

"How long have you felt as if you were missing something?"

"For a long time."

"How long?"

"As long as I can remember."

"You know, Henry, the Book of Proverbs says, 'The heart knows its own bitterness.'[1] Can you get in touch with your heart and try to recall when you began to sense there was something missing?"

"I'm not sure; I don't know how to do that."

"I'll try to help you. Did it start with the trips to the hospital for your condition?"

"Maybe it did, but it's so long ago I can't remember."

"Tell you what, describe the feelings that you wrestle with when you consider that something was missing."

"I can tell you where I feel it when it hurts."

"Where does it feel painful?"

"It's like it's on my chest."

"What does that pain feel like on your chest?"

"Like I am struggling to catch my breath."

"Henry, sometimes our hearts carry pain because we have buried it so deep that we lose our ability to describe what that pain feels like. Try to describe the feeling to me in a picture. Perhaps we may discover something that can turn on a light in a dark place you can't remember or don't want to revisit. Maybe this will help you get in touch. Let's say I was five years old, I was your son, and I wanted you to explain to me what the hurt felt like so that I could understand it. What kind of picture would you use to describe that hurt and pain to me?"

"Oh, I can do that. I feel like I am lying on the sand at the bottom of the ocean floor under all that water. I can't move or breathe, even though I need to, because there is a sunken battleship that is sitting on my chest. I can't move it, and I can't get out from under it to catch my breath."

"Whoa! That's some kind of pain, Henry! How long have you felt as if you were on the ocean floor, unable to breathe or move because a sunken battleship was resting on your chest?"

"For years."

"Henry, when you first said you felt pain I had no idea that it was so intense. How many years has this battleship been there?"

In a moment, Henry paused and became very quiet. Suddenly, as he finally realized that his heart was trying to tell him something, his face brightened. He said, "You know, when I was about thirteen or fourteen years old, I was studying fractions in math. My teacher got frustrated with me because I wasn't getting it. She made a statement to me that crushed me. She said, 'Why aren't you getting it? Are you stupid or something?' At that moment, I felt really confused and totally crushed."

"You mean as though a battleship were sitting on your chest?"

"Exactly! But it got worse."

"How so?"

"Well, because I had gone through treatments for my epilepsy while growing up, I was faced again with the possibility that something was wrong with me. The teacher's words reinforced the idea that maybe I was mentally lacking because of the illness, or maybe I just wasn't smart. I know now that's not true."

"So what made the pain worse?"

"Well, my brother was a math expert, so the teacher and my dad asked him to tutor me. During one of my tutoring sessions, my brother got really frustrated with me and shouted the same words that the teacher had used, 'Why aren't you getting it? Are you stupid or something?'"

"You mean he used the exact phrase that the teacher did?"

"Exactly!"

"How did that make you feel?"

"Well, I really looked up to my brother, and when he said that, I was crushed!"

"You mean crushed like a battleship was on your chest?"

"Exactly!"

"So, how long have you felt the pain and hurt that we've talked about, Henry?"

"Ever since that incident in school. What made it worse was that my dad sided with my brother. From then on I was determined to prove to everyone that I wasn't stupid."

Tears flowed from Henry's eyes as his heart opened up and he faced the deep sense of self-doubt rooted in that incident. His painful self-doubt had been submerged under the ocean of his life's voyage, pinned beneath a battleship of mammoth proportions.

"Since then, I have felt that I had to prove that I wasn't what they said I was. And ever since then, I have felt that even the people who should have believed in my capabilities haven't believed in them."

"So, ever since then you have gone through the same situation, only with different people and under different circumstances?"

"Correct!" This is one of Henry's favorite words. I guess because he believes everything has to be.

"So then, somebody sunk your battleship, like in the Milton Bradley game?"

"You got it!"

"Except you're pinned under the bottom of it all and can't get any relief—so you can't get this thing off your chest?"

"Correct!"

"And the place where you feel the weight is on your chest where your heart is?"

Illumination lit up Henry's face in one of those flashes of insight sometimes called a "eureka" moment. We decided we were going to get the weight of those memories off of his chest because they had been deeply anchored in his heart and were causing him to doubt himself.

Hope is experienced at a feeling level in the soul and is triggered by memories in our imaginations. If our memories are disappointing, then our hopes are not active.

Memory and hope are inseparable. We build our hopes through life most often by the remembrance of past successes or the dream to overcome past failures. Either way our imaginations are built upon the foundation of our memories. If you have had little success in building energizing memories based on affirming life experiences, your hope for the future can be weak or even nonexistent. Your blocks from the past need to be reconciled and removed.

Often when I am helping individuals sort through life issues, they arrive at an important moment. The wounded person comes to a point where he is ready to allow the love of God into the painful areas of his life. Henry was at just such a place.

Henry and I had a time of healing prayer, and I asked God to touch him at the point of that crushing pain buried in his heart. The car filled with the healing presence of God.

In a moment of safety, honesty and surrender, Henry found freedom in the tears streaming down his face. Those tears were beginning to dissolve the mountain of doubt that had blocked and blurred his vision about himself. He had doubted himself because of the words and actions of significant others who were older and who knew better than he did. He perceived them as having great authority, and it caused his heart to sink under the crushing pain of a massive battleship, pinning him to the bottom of the world.

Henry's eyes were still closed when I asked him if he was ready to cancel out the debt the teacher and his older brother owed him and to dump the files of his internal computer. Since they could not pay him back for the damage that was done, and since he had been demanding payback for their insensitivity throughout his life and relationships, he was working off the debt himself.

Henry's problem was that he was trying to disprove a lie about himself to himself. Doing this is like taking a loan from the Mafia. The interest rate is so high that no matter how much you pay back, you will owe them money for the rest of your life. Enough is never enough. You will never feel good enough about yourself to merit letting yourself off the hook.

When people label you, devalue you or challenge your sense of self-worth without separating who you are from what you do, they leave a residue of deep self-doubt in their wake. That self-doubt accumulates with each passing day and each passing event. A system of belief and a deep mental model about how the world works and how you work in it form and embed themselves in the ocean of your soul.

If that sabotaging belief system goes undetected, as it did in Henry's case, it causes that deep doubt to drive you to prove your worth, or disprove your lack of worth, to everyone in your path. We will take an in-depth look at these powerful belief systems later on in this book.

The depth of your heart is the place from which all of your life originates. If you don't know what is stuck at the depths, you will never know what is possible at the heights. Your self-doubt causes you to get buried on the ocean floor of your hopes and dreams where you cannot see the light of day or breathe the air of freedom. The ocean, which is designed to support life on the surface, now drowns you under its awesome power.

Henry realized that his teacher and his brother, in an uncanny fashion, both confirmed the same lie. Whatever the motivating factor was behind the teacher's derogatory comment, it was the same power that moved his older brother. Although they posed it in a question, the message to his heart was the same: "You are stupid and incapable."

Henry spent so many years thinking at the surface and never getting in touch with his deep pain and inner conflict that he often drove too fast, took charge when it wasn't his place and reacted in anger and self-defense. After all those years he was still trying to prove to his teacher and his brother that he did get it and that he wasn't stupid. Little did he realize that he was really trying to prove these things to himself. The irony was that neither his brother nor his teacher was present any longer. Nevertheless, they remained alive and well in the painful memory that refused to die.

Once the light went on and Henry saw his teacher and his brother in that light, he was able to release them from the debt they owed him. Forgiveness is about releasing others from the debt we demand for the things they robbed from us. While others were responsible for their actions toward Henry, he was responsible for spending his energy demanding that life pay him back through his needs-driven behavior.

Holding on to the right to be right never gets us what we want from those who have wronged us. It only invites successive similar situations to be added to the column of debt until the balance owed becomes larger than the national debt.

The Pathway of Doubt

Once Henry released his brother and teacher for being responsible for his present pain, he realized that he had made choices as well. Again and again Henry chose to believe that what his teacher and brother said was true even though what they had said took place in years past. Henry came to hear everything as nonaffirming. He processed and felt every negative experience as the voice of a former teacher and an older brother. He came to experience on the outside what he had repeated to himself all along on the inside.

We tend to experience what we choose to believe is true even if it is not that way at all. We filter everything that comes to us through the lens of our perceptions based on our total life experiences. What we perceive determines what we conceive or to what we give birth in our lives. If we believe, for example, that since one person devalues us, everyone who speaks about issues in our lives is devaluing us, then we conceive or give birth to the experience of rejection over and over again. We also give birth to a defensive posture that closes us to hearing truth.

The power of self-doubt in Henry's life was not caused by the belittling words of his teacher and brother. The power of their words stemmed from a belief in Henry that was formed by his bout with an illness, his struggle with math and by not feeling good enough for the world in which he lived.

Henry was aware that somewhere in that painful world he had a part to play in the drama that had unfolded. At some level he had given off signals that invited others to go after him in the same way that an angry dog smells fear in an individual and uses it to its advantage.

What we refuse to face is attracted to us in increasingly greater ways. Bitter roots on a tree lead to bitter fruits. Bitter judgments from our past lead to bitter expectations of our future.

I suppose trying to get a battleship off your chest is as big a challenge as trying to cast a mountain into the sea. All of us arrive on the planet with a destiny ahead of us that requires diligence and effort to fulfill. Some find it easier than others to progress along the path of their destiny. Regardless of the pace at which we learn and grow, there are struggles and hurtles unique to each soul that have to be faced and overcome whether we were born in a palace or a pit.

Henry grew up within the cultural and economic boundaries of an inner-city neighborhood and within the limitations of inner-city relationships with friends and family. The perceived limitations of his childhood created a self-concept that left him feeling handicapped and even overwhelmed by the seemingly insurmountable odds against him. He despaired of ever becoming competent, well balanced, whole and successful.

Can you can relate to the internal struggles a less-than-perfect environment can create for you? Have you ever felt that you missed opportunities because of the circumstances under which you grew up or have had to live? Have you ever felt that where you were and where you wanted to go were as far apart as the North Pole is from the South Pole?

It's quite possible, depending on how constrained you felt by your environment, that your longings and dreams had no outlet and no expression. When you surveyed where you were as compared to where you were dreaming about going, you could have easily said, "I can't get there from here!" You might have even slipped into a fantasy world to escape the pain of your present moment, telling yourself that someday you would get out of there.

It is also possible that your "someday" never really arrived. For sure, you grew up, left home and pursued your destiny. Yet you have never truly felt free from the restrictions of those early years. Today, your heart might even pine for what your life might have been like if only you could have gotten to where you truly wanted to be. But the deep doubt that is engraved in your memory continues to stand guard at the gate to your dreams, refusing to let you pass.

When Hope Is Held Captive

Effectively or ineffectively, you learned how to survive and how to cope. Some of you may have adopted a cycle of anxiety to cope with the unwanted feelings and perceptions of your limitations. Others may have chosen a "get-even" posture. Whenever you felt those limiting feelings rising up in your heart, you decided that if anyone tried to put the brakes on your dreams, you would put the pedal to the metal and run them over.

Perhaps you found that hiding in a dark place was where you felt safe. From there you could make the world go away and fantasize about being the person you were intended to be. You can spend your entire life hiding from your pain, hiding behind your despair, hiding from the fear of invisibility and hiding from the profound and deep sense of powerlessness that pervades your outlook on the future. Many do.

If you take away people's hope, you take away their sense of safety and security about their tomorrows. When your environment isn't supportive of what you have dreamed and longed to become, you begin to behave like a prisoner of war. A siege mentality occurs when you take the side of your captors and begin to agree with their view of reality. By developing a prisoner-of-war mentality, it becomes increasingly easy to feel comfortable in an environment that denies your capabilities.

Have you come to believe that the negative messages regarding your worth, formed by the destructive circumstances of your formative years, are the truth about you? If you had to learn how to survive growing up, chances are your behavior shifted into a survival mode. You learned how to agree with your captors and say what you needed to say to reduce the stress and pressure you felt.

How can you ever hope to become what you intuitively long to become if all you have ever seen and known is that which cuts you off, shuts you down and treats you as nonexistent? Denial is as old as the human race, and there is always someone or something in our world that wants to put it on you. Finding the resources to fight back and overcome can seem extremely difficult at times.

Nevertheless, it is truly possible to access resources that can support you on your journey toward real and genuine wholeness. I am not talking about mere emotional wholeness. I am talking about becoming all that your heart has ever longed for and your spirit knows is possible—even if your mind reels and staggers at the circumstances that seem to deny those desires.

Doubt is a pervasive presence in the hearts of millions, but it does not have to stay in your heart. Your mountain of doubt may not look like a battleship. It may be a Mack truck or an eighteen-wheeler loaded with garbage at the bottom of a hill. The motor isn't working, and you are standing all alone behind it, trying to push it uphill and getting nowhere fast. Your mountain may be a large redwood tree in a forest of large trees where you are lost and alone. The redwood has fallen on you and pinned you to the ground, and you can't cry out for help. No one can hear you gasping for air and crying for comfort.

Whatever the pictures of the pain in your soul are, they are there trying to tell you something. Learn to face the doubts behind them, and you can come to a place where the mountain can be removed and dumped into the ocean.

My experience with Henry did not end at the point of healing prayer. There was more. Henry's eyes were still closed, and his face was freshly washed with the tears of release and hope that was rebirthed deep in his soul.

Without opening his eyes, he said, "You're not going to believe this!"

"Try me."

"Well, I am seeing another picture of me."

"Go ahead."

"I am sitting on the beach in a large easy chair under the sun, relaxing in the sunshine and enjoying myself. It is a beautiful day."

"Anything else?"

"Yeah. The ocean is calm, and there is a big yacht sitting out in the water."

"Whoa…you mean that the sunken battleship is gone and you're not drowning in your crushing pain? Instead, there is a yacht waiting to set sail for a new adventure?"

"Yes!"

Henry found a level of freedom from his debilitating doubt. As his heart provided him a picture of what transformation was like, he experienced the presence and power of God's freedom, and his countenance changed completely. The tension that had long marked his face was gone. Was he totally free? None of us are totally free from all the residue of a long-held belief system in a moment in time. There is a process that we walk through toward

14

that wholeness. Yet what he did feel, know and experience marked the beginning of Henry's path to wholeness.

Both of us looked out of the windshield at the back of a tanker we were still following as we crawled along the highway in snow and sleet. At that moment Henry and I experienced a meaningful coincidence, or if you prefer, a "God-incident." On the back of the petroleum truck we both saw something that had not been visible to either of us earlier. These words were printed across the bumper: "Smile, God is here!"

I had been sharing during that season of time on being open to the little gifts of meaningful coincidence and serendipity that God often gives when our hearts are open. This was one of those "good and perfect gifts"[2] that came down, signaling us that we were tracking with God and each other. It was an elegant touch that heaven planned to seal an event that was nothing short of an epiphany.

There really is a place where deep doubt can be cleansed from the unknown things that lurk in the shadows of your memory. The dark influence of hidden pain and past disappointment can lose its stranglehold on your sense of worth, your value and your faith for the future. If you are willing to face the challenge, your ears can be opened to hear a voice behind you saying, "This is the way; walk in it."[3] As we journey together through this book, like Henry, you will discover that the mountains of doubt will have to get out of your way! Beyond the shadow of doubt!!

When I had to stop my exploration because the path faded beneath my steps, I found a bottomless abyss at my feet, and out of it comes ... arising I know not from where ... the current which I dare call my life.

—Pierre Teilhard de Chardin

Chapter 2

Finding Healing From the
Robbery of the Spirit

Over the years I have often marveled
Over the years I have often marveled at how some individuals
at how some individuals never seem
never seem to wrestle or battle with doubt. I wish I were more
to wrestle or battle with doubt
like these unflappable souls. They face amazing challenges
seemingly without flinching, while others of us are hurled into
dark seasons of gut-wrenching questioning.

Deep doubt is difficult to acknowledge in ourselves, but it is
nevertheless present. You may not believe that you have deep, hidden doubt, but you probably do. We seldom face the dark layers of
doubt deep within us until a situation or circumstance challenges
us to move beyond our comfort zone.

Deep doubts drive our personalities, motives and actions when
we harbor strong, unmet needs, such as the need for affirmation,

acceptance or approval. The hidden, buried, raw pain of unmet cravings for love and acceptance blocks our pathway to the bright future
promised by God. For when we are not being led by faith and hope,
we are being driven by doubt.

What about you? Are deep doubts that you may not even know
about blocking your path? If you hear enough pep talks on "mountain-moving" by the experts, you might begin to believe that they
live in a world in which every obstacle melts away at the power of
their words. Instead of your faith being built up, you may have
walked away feeling overwhelmed by despair. You have never experienced the things they are talking about, and the cynical voice of
deep doubt mocks, "That's a bunch of nonsense!"

Yet Jesus of Nazareth suggested that living free of doubt was possible. Given the nature of my past experiences, my first response to
that fact would have been, "I doubt it!" Nevertheless, it is truly possible to live our lives free from the dark shadows of doubt that rob
us of our full destinies in Christ.

I think I was born a skeptic as well as a perfectionist, and both
have kept me battling with issues of doubt throughout my journey.
It isn't all that fashionable these days to admit openly that you have
wrestled with doubt. But I believe it is time to open up and examine the things that allow deep doubt to sabotage us.

Have you ever felt that your promises always seemed to lie just
beyond your reach? Perhaps you once started to experience what
you longed for, or you felt certain that you had gotten very close,
only to experience one more frustrating defeat or another aborted
effort. Freeing your destiny from doubt can release you from this
type of self-sabotage.

Everyone wrestles with doubt at one time or another, including
the folks who act as though they have never experienced it. Thank
God there is always a Paul Harvey somewhere ready to tell us the
"rest of the story."

Have you ever wanted to raise your hand and ask for the rest of the story when someone gets up and tells about his or her success? If the teller is more concerned about looking good than about how his words are affecting the listener, he will create discouragement rather than confidence in the hearers. No one is a success overnight. No one gets there without pain and struggle, trial and error and a whole lot of anguish in between. There's a learning curve to every new level we seek to attain in life, and none of it comes without war stories.

The landscape of the human soul can have as many deserts as it has oases. I wish I could tell you that every region of my interior geography looked like Honolulu or Maui. The truth is that some areas of my psyche look like the Wilderness of Sinai, or even the Grand Canyon, complete with snakes and lizards.

I have paid my $39.95 often to those late-night cable-television guys who promise that they can completely turn our lives around. If we purchase their programs, we can have the fancy car, the high-dollar income, the upscale neighborhood, the woman or man of our dreams and even the best-behaved kids on the block. But the only person who actually realizes these benefits is the guy who gets my $39.95.

Thieves and Robbers

Exploring the terrain of the human soul in an effort to see it healed and made whole is the business of any true healer and spiritual practitioner. The One who said, "I have come that you might have life"[1] is all too aware of the thieves and robbers both within and outside the sacred temple of our human souls. Doubt drives us from within, while worldly pressures such as economic need, pressure to produce, pressure to succeed and pressure to fit in and achieve assail us from without. When the robbery is completed, we are left like the man found by the Good Samaritan by the side of the road. We are broken, bloody, bankrupt and alone.

How does Christ come to heal us? Sometimes it takes a whip, a scourge of cords, to cleanse the temple of thieves and robbers. Other times it takes a willingness to experience a period of deconstruction in order to enjoy a season of reconstruction. But all healing will come as faith and hope are rebirthed deep within us.

Birthing Faith and Hope

Jesus was so revolutionary that He threatened the religious systems of His day by His way of seeing the world. He threatened the power of the religious leaders who controlled the people's limited thinking. The religious establishment of His day decided it had only one option. As in the great Hollywood westerns, they said, "This town isn't big enough for the two of us; someone has got to go." Sooner or later there would be a shootout at the "It Ain't OK Corral."

Jesus gained favor with the masses by satisfying their unmet needs. He offered them a new life and gave them the tools and the strategies to attain it. The people tried it and it worked, and overnight the prevailing belief systems of generations that caused the religious leaders to profit from the hopelessness and despair of the masses began to crumble. Jesus awakened in the masses a slumbering hope and a dream of *shalom*, peace that had long been buried under years of disappointment and grief.

This radical new message created an experience of personal empowerment and participation for even the little persons who believed they were nobodies. His actions and His words told the masses that each of their lives was valuable in the grand scheme of things and that they really could make a difference. In the true prophetic spirit, He invited them to imagine a future not yet realized, and He told them that it was within reach, even as close as their right hand.

The people began to clear the cobwebs of their slumbering imaginations and began to envision a future that became increasingly real the more He spoke. His words went off like fireworks on the Fourth of July in their hearts, and they experienced a rebirth of images and symbols that reconnected them to parts of their history that they had forgotten and disowned.

Jesus caused them to feel valued, loved and empowered. He also showed them how to connect with others who were similarly empowered to create a movement that would be nothing less than revolutionary.

Yet the One who came to upset the status quo needed no weapons, only the hearts and spirits of those who were willing to believe that all things are possible. That same deep inner healing is available to you as well. I invite you to join me on a journey, much the same as Henry's, in which you touch places deep inside your heart that you may not have even realized existed. As you experience the healing of wounds hidden deep in your inner man, you will become free in a way you have never imaged— free from deep doubts to be all that God destined you to be. Let's take a look.

Healing the Human Spirit

At the core of my being I am spirit. I am more than matter; I am more than a combination of carbon, hydrogen and oxygen. Because I am made up of both matter and spirit, I touch two worlds at the same time and move in and out of them frequently, even if I am not fully conscious of that fact.

Subconscious Perceptions

There are things that affect me beyond the level of my conscious awareness. There are forces at play that are larger than biological life that I interact with both while I am awake and asleep.

I am influenced at a level of my heart to do and respond according to my perceptions of reality. My perceptions of reality may not always be accurate, yet since they are my perceptions of reality, I tend to always experience what I believe, even if it isn't 100 percent accurate. Let me explain.

Henry deeply held a subconscious memory about himself and mathematical fractions. That long-forgotten yet vivid memory so defined Henry's sense of reality on a subconscious level that it affected everything he did. Yet that memory was not accurate. Henry was not an unintelligent man, but he spent his entire life trying to prove that to himself and everyone else around him in an effort to negate the powerful and dramatic effect of that subconscious memory.

Like Henry, I may believe that I am seeing life clearly, when in actual fact, I am imprisoned in a memory long forgotten that has covered the lens of my vision and projected my inner world onto my outer circumstances.

Henry had to prove to everyone that he was capable, not just with fractions, but also with every other aspect of his life. His deep doubt had become so embedded and anchored within him that instead of moving mountains, he was building bigger ones to block his progress.

Remember this one simple phrase because it tends to prove out in life: You always experience what you believe.

I am reminded of the story of a traveling salesman that was passing into a new area he had not canvassed before. On the way into town, he stopped at a gas station by the side of the road. Sitting outside of the door of the mechanics shop was the owner chewing on a long stalk of grass.

"Howdy, neighbor," the owner of the gas station said.

"Hello," said the salesman. "May I ask you a question?"

"Go right ahead," said the owner.

"How do the folks in this town take to traveling salesmen?"

At which the owner replied with a question: "How did the folks in the last town take to you?"

He said, "Surprisingly well!"

The owner said, "You'll find them the same here!"

At that point the traveling salesman hopped back in his car and drove on into town.

About an hour later another traveling salesman came into town. Invariably he stopped at the gas station and filled up his tank. When the owner of the gas station said hello, the traveling salesman said, "May I ask a question?"

To which the owner readily said, "Go right ahead."

The question he posed was all too familiar: "How do the folks in this town take to a traveling salesman?"

The owner once again answered with a question: "How did the folks in the last town take to you?"

"Not well at all," said the traveling salesman.

And the owner of the gas station promptly said, "You'll find them the same here!"

We always experience what we believe. Our hearts hold deep models and beliefs as to how things work and why they work that way. The heart is all too often the neglected seat of our true intelligence. If there is any hope for change in our experience of reality, it is essential that things change in our hearts.

In the story about Henry, criticism caused deep and pervasive doubt to overshadow and crush his sense of competence. His spiritual immune system was quite depleted at that season in his life for a number of reasons. If you recall, he had struggles with his sense of being loved because his strict father never expressed affection. In addition, he had a physical ailment that created behaviors that required "brain-wave" treatments for a long season in his preadolescent years. The mysterious disappearance of the disease did not alleviate its debilitating effects on his sense of esteem.

Henry's self-esteem was also devastated by thoughtless statements from a teacher he held in high regard and a beloved brother. Their criticism touched his life like an infection that he could not resist. He fought that disease for years, only to find that it had gotten increasingly worse.

That night on Interstate 79, Henry was brought to a moment of epiphany, a turning point. He released his nonaffirming belief and made a radical shift in his view of himself, his life and his relationship to God.

Because Henry had been vulnerable for so many years to the presence and power of doubt, the pressure it had exerted on his soul became a crushing weight that suffocated his creative ability and sapped his joy of living. What he had been told about himself, along with what he believed about himself, formed his concept of himself, or more accurately deformed his self-concept.

It wasn't what the teacher or his brother literally said that was so devastating. It was the silent, more powerful and hidden message that he didn't have the spiritual defenses and spiritual and psychological immune system to deal with. Henry did not hear, "Are you stupid?" He heard, "YOU ARE STUPID!" By the way, there are no mistakes in communication. Even when we couch our message in words that we think will soften the blow, the real communication is what the person feels. The teacher and the elder brother were not speaking, "You are stupid," yet that is exactly what they were saying.

Henry grew up feeling that he was the black sheep of the family because he never got the needed affirmation from his dad, and he always felt that he didn't measure up to the intelligence of his brothers. If it wasn't enough that the authority figures and the heroes in his house weren't affirming, the authority figure in his learning environment offered the same nonaffirming input.

Henry's greater challenge was the inner authority of his own judgments. He lived with a deep sense of self-doubt and felt driven to prove otherwise. He sabotaged his own journey because he was unconscious of what he had accumulated deep below the surface of the water of his soul.

During that icy car trip, Henry took inventory of his life and realized that he had experienced most of it from below the crushing weight of that battleship. The battleship represented an internal image of his hidden self-doubt. He was stuck and could not extricate himself from the weight of it.

On one hand, he attempted to fight against it by always trying to prove himself to everyone around him. Yet on the other hand, he did not have the emotional or spiritual resources with which to fight the good fight of faith. He did not have the spiritual crane and wrecking ball to demolish his doubt. His inaccurate beliefs about himself were cemented into the basement of his heart, and he consciously felt a pervasive sense of being powerless to change. He needed tools.

Tools for Change

You cannot give what you do not have! Today Henry continues to experience increasing levels of healing, and he feels less and less compelled to prove his intelligence or competence. By the power of the Holy Spirit, Henry continues to reconnect to a lost, nonaffirmed part of himself. God is filling that void with more than enough power to keep the battleship off his chest. Henry dumped a mountain of painful internal debris along an interstate in West Virginia in the dead of winter, and then he saw clearly enough to be able to smile, because God was there.

To live without a doubt, beyond the shadows of uncertainty, requires some tools and some skills, as well as an ability to see some things you may not have known about yourself.

Let's see if we can put some tools in your hand and then help you develop the skills to use those tools so you can reclaim what has been stolen. When we get through, you might find that just ahead of you on the highway of life is a "tanker full of oil" (the oil of joy perhaps). You may also joyfully discover that the tanker is leading you away from hidden pain and shadowy doubt to a new future, reminding you to "smile," because "God is here!"

In the next chapter, I invite you to come along with me on an internal journey in which I uncover some fears that were submerged in the ocean of my own soul as well as some powerful weapons to defeat them.

How we are educated by children . . . We live

in currents of universal reciprocity.

—MARTIN BUBER

Chapter 3

Dredging Up Hidden Fears

The Gulf Coast of Florida is absolutely
breathtaking on a clear morning, and
from the balcony of a five-star resort

The Gulf Coast of Florida is absolutely breathtaking on a clear morning, and from the balcony of a five-star resort hotel room, it's the picture-perfect shot that travel agencies use to sell vacation packages. The waters beckoned us to come with every breaking wave and current that hit the shoreline.

The kids wanted to get out on the open Gulf and go for a boat ride. The distance between our dream and our desired outcome was only a few miles (just as we are much closer than we realize to most things in life that we really want and desire). The sun was already heating up the day and was well on its way to the highest position in the sparkling blue sky by eleven in the morning.

As the crow flies, we could have been at the marina in about two minutes. But unlike the Flintstones, we had no pterodactyl-sized crows to fly us from our balcony to the marina. So, the next best thing was to call the concierge's desk for directions and request that our car be brought to the front of the hotel.

We began to take a rather circuitous route to get to where we wanted to be. Most roads and highways are of necessity built according to the lay of the land because human energy takes the path of least resistance. "You can't get there from here" was probably first said by a frustrated highway engineer who kept uncovering obstacles as he attempted to create a new route to solve a city's traffic snarl.

It's like that for all of us when we try to pursue new objectives and achieve new outcomes. We discover that we "can't get there from here" because obstacles are blocking our way. Too often we settle for the path of least resistance. It involves the least amount of hassle, and although it seems to take longer to get to where we want to be, at least it circumvents our having to overcome things that seem impossible to surmount.

We learn in life to wait patiently for our dreams, to take things in stride. But somewhere deep inside is a longing for the realization of our dream. All the delays of going around the hard stuff can make our dream feel illusive, as it if will never come.

We arrived in the lobby of the resort to discover that the valet attendants the night before had failed to turn off the headlights on our vehicle, thus draining the battery. We were dreaming of being in the glistening water, but the unexpected delay in experiencing the fulfillment of our dream added at least thirty minutes to our frustration. Refusing to be deterred, we politely asked the attendants to take care of jump-starting the vehicle since the problem was created by their oversight. They kindly agreed to take care of the mishap, and we proceeded to the marina, only mildly rustled by the inconvenience.

There were three boats sitting at the dock waiting for someone to rent them, each with a decent outboard motor that could open up on the open water at about sixty miles per hour. We were now only two miles from the Gulf of Mexico; however, the rules did not allow us to create a wake. Therefore, moving at almost idle speed would take us an additional thirty minutes to get out onto that inviting water. We could not see our dream from where we were, but could only picture the refreshing view from the balcony in our memories.

The kindly gentlemen who operated the marina moved quite slowly. I have discovered that life on Florida's southwest Gulf Coast is like a setting on an old Victrola. If you can remember, the Victrola had a lever with four different settings. We used three of those settings, yet never had the opportunity to use the fourth unless we wanted to have fun and mess up one of our records. Albums played at 33⅓ rpm, singles played at 45, and a few family albums played at 78. But the fourth speed was something like 16. For fun we would sneak a record at that speed and laugh and laugh when the voices slowed down to the point of being almost motionless. Well, that was about how quickly the man moved and spoke on our anxious way to our "dream."

For a native New Yorker, that pace is a major culture shock, and everything in me wanted to finish his sentences and do his job so that I could get on with my vacation before it was over.

When the kindly gentlemen finally released us to our objective, we idled out of the dock, down toward the cove and turned right into a canal area. Once out of sight of the marina, the engine began to make a funny noise and a bell began to sound—and no amount of button pressing or praying would make it stop. We had rented a cell phone in case of an emergency, so now I was explaining to the same man that something strange was happening that was getting in the way of my desired future.

Speaking slowly, contemplatively and perhaps even philosophically, the man explained that it could be any one of a number of things. After hearing the list, which took another four minutes, I asked him what we needed to do. The thing I greatly feared came upon me. I was told I would have to turn around, take the boat back and start all over again with another boat.

Have you ever had one of those days? By this time, the picture from the balcony of our beautiful resort hotel room had turned from a dream into a nightmare. It dawned on me that this pursuit of the open water was not going to take place according to my schedule. But in life, deeper lessons can be learned through our detours, and they are only preparations for the greater lessons to be learned on the high seas of human adventure.

We returned the ill-fated motorboat to the dock and exchanged it for another one whose gas gauge was broken and did not register how much fuel we actually had in the tank. Again and again the gracious man reassured us that we had enough. But visions of stalling out in the middle of the Gulf during an afternoon thunderstorm flooded my brain, and twinges of anxiety began to rise from my soul into my chest. But I already knew there was no convincing this guy to rethink his choice for a better boat, so I smiled, backed up from the dock and launched out once again for the open sea.

As a young kid I dreamed of great adventures all the time. Whether at sea or on a mountain, in the air or on dry land, I longed to risk everything for some great cause, some noble effort or some incredible act of courage and feat of strength. I grew up watching *Wide World of Sports* on Saturdays and vicariously seeing myself in the accomplishments of the sports heroes.

Dreams and Imaginations

When your dream is only in your imagination, you can convince yourself that the distance between the television and a downhill skiing trophy or first place on the high dive is negligible. The "thrill of victory" captured my imagination, and I tended to ignore the "agony of defeat" part of the story. I didn't want anyone to tell me that while Babe Ruth was the home-run king, he had struck out far more times at bat than he actually had hit home runs.

Kids do not have to reconcile a lot of past history that gets in their way of believing for the impossible. They do not doubt their own potential or capabilities because they haven't experienced failure as a liability. In a normal situation, children fall many times while learning to walk. Such failures only strengthen their sense of determination.

As a child growing up in the city, I had visions of swinging on a tire tube attached to a long hemp rope, hanging from a large branch of a tree that hovered over a swimming hole. At the right moment, I would let go of the rope and tube and fling myself into the refreshing water below, emerging to do it again and again. Yet I heard a ton of negative and fearful messages from the time I was little. Those messages anchored themselves deeply in my soul. Until at a moment of opportunity, like an uninvited guest showing up in a conversation, a voice inside me would rehearse those messages and challenge my confidence.

I was fourteen years old and was sitting at the edge of a dock at a large lake in upstate New York. Off to my right in the distance was a tire tube tied to a long rope, hanging from a large tree branch that stretched out over a side of the lake where the water was about fifteen feet deep. This same internal uninvited guest began voicing those undermining messages.

Fear had taken root deep within my psyche, and self-doubt was its bedfellow. I stood there frozen looking into the brown water. I was not consciously aware of how much of an effect certain messages had on my experience of reality, and I was not fully aware of why I froze at the opportunity to do what I dreamed of when I was younger. Real lake water with real fish was different from the lake water I had imagined while sitting in my living room watching a TV image of a young boy doing exactly what I knew I could do. I had not counted on the real thing being different from what I had imagined.

Once I got to the lake, I saw how deep the water was. Even though I knew how to swim, the water was not clear like the water in my cousin's pool. There in three feet of water and a twenty-foot round tank I had experienced incredible adventures all over the world's lakes and oceans.

I also heard negative and fearful messages of young people who had drowned. It seemed as though bad news riveted itself to my soul as well as the collective soul of my family.

The water in the lake looked dirty. The bottom wasn't a blue plastic lining; instead it was layered in rocks and soil. Strange-looking bugs skimmed the surface of the water, and funny-looking things crawled on the plants under the water. This was a different world, an unknown world that did not operate by rules I understood, and my imagination hadn't counted on such things.

I faced the fact that at fourteen I doubted my ability to handle the world of tire tubes on ropes over swimming holes. I had to make an adjustment in my view of reality. What my imagination had perceived about swimming holes and tire tubes was not inaccurate. It just wasn't complete.

I stood watching other boys do what I really wanted to do, swinging over the water and plunging in. I felt my heart take the plunge with them. But when my turn came, doubt and fear gripped me as tightly as I gripped the rope. I couldn't let go, and neither did the uninvited guest inside me. I marveled at the freedom of the others. They were able to let go of the rope at the right moment and enjoy the thrill as they plunged into the murky water. I wanted to follow. But I could not get beyond the shadows of my doubts that darkened my view to what was real and what was possible.

Touching Our Dream

The boat engine sputtered and nudged me back from my thoughts. After thirty minutes of navigating our way through the canals and bays, we made a right turn, and there beyond the rocks was the Gulf of Mexico. Here, the water was pretty clear and only ten to fifteen feet deep, while just beyond the rocks we couldn't see the bottom because it was so deep. There seemed to be a whole lot going on beneath the surface.

After many delays and setbacks, we were at the threshold of what we had dreamed about from the balcony of our hotel room. I was not a kid anymore, and I was sitting behind the wheel of what looked like a big boat at the marina. But now, compared to the open Gulf, I felt small and our boat looked like a little toy. I held on to the steering wheel tightly as I began to experience the same feelings that I had at fourteen sitting on that dock, wrestling with whether or not I wanted to plunge into the water or turn and run.

My kids were excited; there was no sense of apprehension—they were just having a good time. Yet Dad was feeling this incredible anxiety because the water was a lot more active outside the bay in the open Gulf. There was a moderate chop, and I was at the helm of the ship.

A "moderate chop" is a meteorologist's definition of water conditions that sounds a lot more "moderate" than it feels when you are actually in it. It's like hearing a pilot, who lives and breathes flying, come over the plane's PA system encouraging you to stay calm at forty thousand feet during moderate turbulence. You listen to his voice as your white knuckles tightly grip your seat because your soda just ended up on the ceiling and your stomach felt as if it just hit the floor. It certainly depends on how you interpret reality. You interpret your reality, and then you experience it accordingly.

The sight of that wide-open sea has doubtless sent sparks of inspiration through the hearts of the seafaring and adventurous. Yet my fears were immediately present, together with my sense of incompetence about handling rough waters and the threat of something going wrong while we were too far out in the water to swim to shore. In the face of that immense Gulf, I felt totally at the mercy of the elements.

Navigating Through Doubt

Doubt flooded my mind. I doubted my ability to manage what seemed to be beyond my management skills. My doubts blocked my path. I did not know if I wanted to enter into what I had dreamed about only a short while ago. From my vantage point I could turn my head slightly to the right and see the balcony of my hotel room. From that balcony I had no conscious apprehensions, doubts or fears. From that perspective it was safe to dream. Yet now, surrounded by deep blue sea, things began to surface, not from the depths of the Gulf, but from the depths of my unconscious. Fears and doubts that had been hiding from conscious view were now floating like debris on the surface of my consciousness.

The human spirit is like deep waters, and it takes someone of understanding to draw out of us what we may not even know is really there. I was caught with nowhere to run or hide, but my children were excited about what lay ahead. They innocently and beautifully experienced the Gulf of Mexico for its marvelous inspiration and power.

We tend to not take time to get to know ourselves very well. It can be quite frightening to face the depths of the human psyche. We prefer amusement and distraction to contemplation and reflection. We will go a certain distance for holistic health, but beyond detoxing our bodies we do not seek opportunities to detox our psyches.

As I looked into the beautiful Gulf of Mexico, it reflected back to me my fears. Just as debris that was tossed overboard by a careless vacationer floated on the water, up out of the depth of my deep heart floated debris that littered the landscape of my soul. Everywhere I looked I seemed to encounter the mirrors of my deep soul.

The litter and the debris that came from someone's hunger for another bottle of soda, another smoke or another bottle of booze marred the Gulf's beauty and detracted from its glory. It wasn't the kind of stuff that can be recycled on the ocean floor and transformed into something beneficial. Cleaning up the debris that can't be recycled from the ocean of our souls can be a tough job. Yet this kind of work is necessary because debilitating doubts and fears pollute the soul.

Our spirits are a vast resource of possibility and potential. Yet often they have been polluted by our drives to satisfy our unmet needs with things that do not truly satisfy, muddying the waters of clear insight and perception, preventing us from becoming everything we were meant to become. Our intuitive faculties, our imaginations and our memories have become impaired, and our senses have become dull and deprived of their full capabilities. All of this is due to the things that we and others have dumped into the waters of our inner souls.

We have lost our senses. We have come under the power of elemental spirits that reduce us to slaves rather than heirs. We have become ensnared by policy and politics at every level of our existence from healthcare to education. Our hearing has become impaired because too many inauthentic voices vie for our attention and take away our sense of hope and possibility of empowerment. Our vision has become blurred because too many false images have blinded our sight to true greatness. Our sense of discernment has suffered so that, much like the effects of a cold or flu, we have lost our ability to smell as well as taste. Without the ability to "smell" we cannot distinguish that which is a pleasant aroma from that which carries the scent of death.

As vast as the Gulf of Mexico really was when we were out on that ship, a floating bottle of Jack Daniel's with a bit of the poison left in it had the ability to rob the air of the pure smell of salt water. It sent mixed messages into the atmosphere. In the same way, the fears and doubts that live within us pollute not merely the waters of our psyches, but the air around them as well, and they send mixed messages to our perception of reality.

Sailing Through Spiritual Debris

Great possibilities exist for us when we eliminate deep doubt from the ocean of our hearts. The fears, doubts and painful memories that are dumped in the vast resource of our internal depths don't just affect us at the surface of our consciousness. Deep below, at the subconscious level, our emotional, psychological and spiritual debris has power to kill our souls. How much sea life has been destroyed because we dumped beer bottles, plastic garbage bags, cans and other trash into our waterways and oceans, assuming that it would just take care of itself? Instead, a harvest of death resulted to the sea life that lives in harmony below the surface of the waters.

Once spiritually toxic debris is dumped into the deep realms of our internal ocean, death occurs. Hope and childlike innocence that confidently embrace and enjoy each moment die under the toxic death of suffocating debris. While sitting at the helm of that twenty-foot Sea Ray, I was forced to deal with the contradictions in my soul for the sake of my children. In doing so, I found a new outcome that did not allow doubt or fear to get in the way of my future.

Finding New Outcomes

As our tiny vessel drifted toward the giant sky, my thoughts began to drift once again as well. Looking at the bright faces of my boys, I was reminded of a moment much earlier in my life when I was about their age. Growing up in West Brighton, I spent my summer days and spring afternoons playing knock-hockey, kickball and basketball at a popular playground and park. The park had high slides for bigger kids and high swings that even adults enjoyed. It was like a home away from home. I got along with everyone and became close friends with the head attendant of the park, who taught me how to play Ping-Pong and shuffleboard.

Those days were full of fun and free from conflict, until one day a person I considered a friend decided that he did not want me to be with him at the knock-hockey table. Rather than cause a fuss, I moved to another part of the park and started to climb the high slide to enjoy a few rides. This "friend"—Sandy—met me at the bottom of the slide and told me that he didn't want me there either.

I was generally peaceful by nature and didn't like conflict. But when he threatened me, I got angry and told him what I thought about his bullying behavior. He responded by punching me in my solar plexus and knocking the wind out of me for the first time in my life. It was a frightening experience, and when I couldn't catch my breath, I doubled over and fell on the concrete. He then demanded that I leave the park, which demand, due to my fear, my bruise from the fall and the pain I felt, I obeyed rather quickly.

My dad's business office was up the street a little way, and I walked through the door red-faced, bruised, with tears running down my cheeks and gasping for breath. My dad, who had a tendency to overprotect me, began to panic. I told him that Sandy had just punched me in the stomach really hard and kicked me out of the park.

Dad got angry and threatened to go tell Sandy a thing or two and to call his grandmother, who was a chronically complaining customer of my father's. She griped continually about the cost of home heating fuel. (My dad owned a business involving fuel oil.) Dad muttered some words in Italian, a few I knew to be less than flattering and one or two that were expletives. (Because this was his worst customer's grandson, I think he wanted to tell them both off.) He stood up from behind his desk and moved to the front door of the office where I was standing looking like a whipped puppy.

At the precise moment that my dad stood up, Uncle Danny, the youngest of my dad's brothers and who was at the office on a lunch break, intercepted him. "Don't do that," he said as he blocked him from coming to me. I wanted Dad to rescue me from my fears and to fix Sandy's wagon. But Uncle Danny, who never walked away from a fight in his life, wanted me to face my mountain of fear myself.

Uncle Danny looked a lot like Michael Landon. He was handsome and a real macho ladies' man. He lifted weights and was about 275 pounds of pure muscle. His biceps were like large grapefruits, and he was terrifying just to look at. When Uncle Danny meant business, nobody messed with him.

Uncle Danny could not stand the thought of having a weakling nephew in the Chironna clan. He quickly grabbed my upper arm and "escorted"[1] me back to the playground where he stood at the entrance, surveyed the landscape, spotted Sandy and then turned to me and said, "There he is. Now go and fight back!"

Fear struck me at the core of my being. I had taken one blow to the stomach; I didn't think I had the stuff to handle another one. I tried to argue with him and then pleaded, yet Uncle Danny's presence and stature prevented me from getting around him. He told me we were not going back to the office until I won the fight. I realized that I had a choice: I could fight Uncle Danny, or I could confront Sandy. I would have less pain with the latter choice.

I sheepishly walked down the stairs to the first level of the park where there were benches, swings and seesaws. I approached the knock-hockey table, and Sandy looked up and saw me returning. He dropped his knock-hockey stick and spewed out threats as he moved toward me.

My heart was in my throat, and my feet began to turn back toward the entrance to the park. Lifting my eyes I saw Uncle Danny standing in a pose like Superman with his fists on his hips and his legs firmly planted about three feet apart on the ground. The only difference between Superman and Uncle Danny was that Superman's face wore a smile. Uncle Danny had one of those threatening "if looks could kill" faces. I knew that if I did not deal with Sandy, Uncle Danny would deal with me.

Choosing the lesser of two evils, my feet and eyes quickly turned back in the direction of Sandy, who now stood boldly right in front of me. He threatened to hit me again and mocked me for coming back for more. Then he hauled back and hit me again in my upper body a few times, and it hurt. But something else happened while he was hitting me. I got mad at myself for allowing him to do it.

All of a sudden I started swinging back with no particular style or sense of direction. Surprisingly, two of my punches landed one after another, the first to Sandy's gut, knocking the wind out of him, and the second to his nose, making it bleed.

Wow, what a sense of power! I felt like a lion and was ready to finish the job. But instead of hitting him again, I went over to his pride and joy, his bicycle. I threw it down a nearby flight of stairs that led to the basketball courts. Then I turned around and said to him in the most authoritative voice I ever used, "Don't ever mess with me again. It's time for you to get on your bike and get out of the park!" He did so willingly and quickly!

I walked back up the entrance to the park, a bit ruffled and worn, yet victorious and feeling like a champion. Uncle Danny beamed; he was proud of me. When we got back to the office and I recounted the entire event blow by blow, Dad got angry with his younger brother for encouraging me to fight. Yet in my heart, I knew that Uncle Danny had shown me that there was more to me than I had realized. He had given me a gift, a shining moment of self-discovery.

Years later in graduate school studying theology, I went through what the mystics of old called "the dark night of the soul," a time in which I felt totally alone and abandoned by God. If that wasn't bad enough, I also felt the oppressive presence of evil forces seeking to bring my soul to the depths of despair and depression. I cried out for help, and no help seemingly came. I had no idea what was going on, and I wanted to close my mind to the madness that seemed to drown me in sorrow. All my doubts and fears loomed larger than life, and I felt attacked by demons. I remember falling to the floor in agony, depression and despair and crying out for help from God. At a moment when I thought I was about to sink and never resurface, I heard a voice (not audible) deep within my spirit rise up and say, "Remember Sandy Harris."[2] All of a sudden God looked a lot like Uncle Danny, and the oppression I was enduring looked a lot like Sandy.

I got up to my feet and found something deeper than my pain, deeper than my fears and deeper than my doubts. I began to hear my own voice speaking with authority, reclaiming my right to existence and to the abundant life promised by God. I declared before heaven and hell that I was not going to be subject to these terrors any longer. Immediately I felt a surge of energy move from my gut through my lungs and into my mouth. There was a power in my words that literally cleansed the atmosphere both in and around me from the dark forces that were oppressing me.

I resurfaced from that deep dark pit with a new sense of purpose and power. I had just been given a dynamic key that opened a new door to my life and a powerful weapon that pushed those hellish forces back and out of my way.

That spiritual battle actually awakened dormant possibilities lying deep within my soul that had not been fully aroused since that memorable day in the park. I have since realized that there are defining moments when persons or circumstances block the pathway to our purpose. These individuals or circumstances can cause our fears and doubts to resurface, dredging them up from the darkest depths of our souls. When this happens we need to face our fears head-on.

I have also discovered that the Hound of Heaven may come upon the scene in much the same way as Uncle Danny did, forcing us to confront face to face what we have been running from: our fears and doubts about ourselves and about God. And just like Uncle Danny, Jesus Christ will stand there beside us and demand that we stop running, turn around, confront our adversary and fight until we win.

Crossing Over New Thresholds

I can relate to the phrase, "Conflicts without, fears within."[3] Oftentimes when we cross over into new and unexplored territory in life, we find distress as opposed to relief and relaxation. The edge of adventure is sharp and can pierce through to the internal conflicts that divide our souls between our hopes and our fears.

When we cross over new thresholds, we need to also shatter old structures and patterns that have prevailed in our minds and hearts. In this way we allow our inner man to be cleansed so that we can gain the promise of new outcomes.

Salvador Dali said, "The difference between false memories and true ones is the same as for jewels; it is always the false ones that look most brilliant!"[4] Our inability to see and perceive our desires clearly is due to the false brilliance of former setbacks that became deeply embedded in our subconscious. Eventually they settle in and take root, choking out our hope and desire.

The pure in heart are able to see God. They have no splits in their consciousness; therefore, they have no limits to their vision. The childlike innocence of my sons served as an important parable and lesson when we were out in the Gulf of Mexico. As our tiny vessel plowed through choppy water, even though they had never been out on the open sea, they innocently experienced the unexpected with unrestrained joy. They giggled and cheered, affirming the unexpected. At the same time, I was anticipating that one of the waves that was rocking us back and forth might flip us over at high speeds.

Boats are made for rough water, and children are made for innocently affirming the unexpected with excitement and laughter. There on the choppy seas of adventure I was getting an object lesson all around me of the need to be cleansed of the deep fears that create sabotaging doubt.

I want to assist you, to help you navigate your way to your hopes and dreams by inviting you to uncover your fear. For it is fear that often sabotages your best efforts at success by creating deep uncertainty in your soul. You can learn to rise on waves of possibility and reach heights of confidence, even when negative and dark circumstances loom large on the horizon of your desires and threaten your vision of the future. Can you really can live a life free from deep uncertainty and fear? Can you can approach your future with the confidence that even mountains will have to get out of your way? Beyond the shadow of doubt!

Section II

Shadows That Create the Blocks

Beyond
the
Shadow
of
Doubt

Beyond
the
Shadow
of
Doubt

There is a time when passing through a light that you walk in your own shadow.

—Keri Hulme

Chapter 4

Chasing Shadows of
Inner Conflict

Even our own children's fairy tales
tell us truths about the human
condition. For Peter Pan, who "lost"

Even our own children's fairy tales tell us truths about the human condition. For Peter Pan, who "lost" his shadow, catching it required entering the second floor balcony door of Wendy's bedroom where he not only reunited with his shadow, but he also made some new friends. His shadow's strange behavior led him unknowingly into a new future.

Shadows are interesting things in that they resemble us, yet they cast only an outline and are always in the dark. There is no depth to a natural shadow because it is flat. Yet it mimics all our movements and is patterned after us. Like long shadows that fall on a sidewalk in the late afternoon, our shadows can loom larger than we are. At times, depending upon where the sunlight is hitting our frame, our shadows can stand at a unique angle and appear to be in front of us instead of behind us, leading us instead of following. They can behave in mischievous ways, doing the exact opposite of what we expect.

The shadowy part of us—a dimension of ourselves that all of us need to deal with, by the way—is usually some aspect of ourselves that we have ignored, wished would go away, rejected, scorned or refused to acknowledge. It's the part of us that we wish was not around, and it's the part of us that shows up at the most embarrassing moments to humiliate us. Since our shadows are a part of our identities, we cannot blame their dark images on the devil and seek an exorcist. We cannot snap our fingers or wave our hand and make these shadows disappear.

These shadows are found in the valley of death. In one of the most dramatic paradoxes of the Christian faith, Christ told His disciples that to find their lives they must lose them.[1] In essence, He said that we must die in order to live. We need to die to self to come alive to God and to genuinely loving relationships.

The psalmist David spoke of this place in the Twenty-third Psalm when he said, "Even though I walk through the valley of the shadow of death."[2] Shadows are dark reflections of the pain that hides in the depths of our souls. The valley is our journey that provides many opportunities to stop running away from the parts of us that give us pain. Sooner or later we all have to pass through that region in the swampland of the soul and face the things we have hidden in dark places. What we refuse to face cannot be erased.

The Gift of Pain

Pain is a gift not to be ignored. If I am in pain, it is an indication that I need to look at something in my heart. Even if I am not the cause of my pain, whatever or whoever caused it triggered something in me. The pain is telling me something. In the North, if I stay out in the bitter cold too long and ignore the pain in my hands and feet until I can't feel it anymore, I may end up with frostbite. That frostbite could become gangrene, and I might lose my fingers or toes. Those extremities would never again cause me pain in the cold.

The victim of frostbite learns that to avoid pain is to avoid life. Emotional pain works in much the same way. Avoiding the things that trigger emotional pain in us does not rid us of the roots of our pain. It merely masks the pain so that we can deceive ourselves into thinking it does not exist. Affliction and adversity are a part of the human experience, and pain often provides opportunities to become more compassionate and merciful toward others who are enduring hardships.

Asaph, the chief musician under King David of Israel, once foolishly commented that evil people experienced no pain. Listen to his words, and see how he needed to face his own shadows:

> No doubt about it! God is good—
>> good to good people, good to the good-hearted.
> But I nearly missed it,
>> missed seeing his goodness.
> I was looking the other way,
>> looking up to the people
> At the top,
>> envying the wicked who have it made,
> Who have nothing to worry about,
>> not a care in the whole wide world.
>
> Pretentious with arrogance,
>> they wear the latest fashions in violence,
> Pampered and overfed,
>> decked out in silk bows of silliness.

They jeer, using words to kill;
   they bully their way with words.
They're full of hot air,
   loudmouths disturbing the peace.
People actually listen to them—can you believe it?
   Like thirsty puppies, they lap up their words.
What's going on here? Is God out to lunch?
   Nobody's tending the store.
The wicked get by with everything;
   they have it made, piling up riches.
I've been stupid to play by the rules;
   what has it gotten me?
A long run of bad luck, that's what—
   a slap in the face every time I walk out the door.

If I'd have given in and talked like this,
   I would have betrayed your dear children.
Still, when I tried to figure it out,
   all I got was a splitting headache...
Until I entered the sanctuary of God.
   Then I saw the whole picture:
The slippery road you've put them on,
   with a final crash in a ditch of delusions.
In the blink of an eye, disaster!
   A blind curve in the dark, and—nightmare!
We wake up and rub our eyes...Nothing.
   There's nothing to them. And there never was.

When I was beleaguered and bitter,
   totally consumed by envy,
I was totally ignorant, a dumb ox
   in your very presence.
I'm still in your presence,
   but you've taken my hand.

You wisely and tenderly lead me,
and then you bless me.

You're all I want in heaven!
You're all I want on earth!
When my skin sags and my bones get brittle,
God is rock-firm and faithful.
Look! Those who left you are falling apart!
Deserters, they'll never be heard from again.
But I'm in the very presence of God—
oh, how refreshing it is!
I've made Lord GOD my home.
God, I'm telling the whole world what you do![3]

It is our pain that tells us where to look for insight and illumination. It guides us to the place where we learn compassion, kindness and tenderheartedness.

Shadows From the Night

Nightmares may seem demonic, but they can be our soul's way of telling us that we have not been facing some dark area in our lives where pain is hidden. We may have ignored that area so long that it might be on the verge of destroying us. Nightmares can actually be gifts in the night that say, "You can't ignore your pain anymore." They can be metaphors and symbols for your pain. You need to deal with this pain, or you will be destroyed by it. Stop ignoring your pain, and pay attention to what it is trying to tell you!

Your internal pain has the power to change you. It can make you touchable, real and genuine, giving you a sense of compassion. *Compassion* comes from a Latin word meaning "to suffer with." Our pain teaches us how to suffer with others in their afflictions.

To avoid our pain and run from our shadows is to refuse a compassionate lifestyle. Avoiding inner pain cuts us off from the land

of the living and causes us to isolate ourselves and deceive ourselves into believing that no one else knows what we are going
through. That's when our shadows lead us into places where we
try to medicate our pain. We start singing that country-western
tune "Make the World Go Away." One of the toughest experiences
we will have is trying to find a way to deal with pain that seems
to have no redemptive purpose at all.

Walter Brueggemann tells us in his work *Finally Comes the Poet* that
many people live with "with layers and layers of alienation that
result from sin, and that are experienced as guilt." Many people
are profoundly burdened with guilt. That guilt, according to
Brueggemann, causes relationships to be driven by subtle brutal-
ity and exploitation.[4] He goes on to say that we do not have to live
in alienation from one another, God or from ourselves. We have a
hope deep within that life can be joyful and blessed.

Brueggeman's words are worthy of consideration:

> Sin characteristically is manifested in distorted relations to
> sex and money, in lust and greed, in abuse of neighbor and
> in the squandering of creation. As the guilt emerges, alien-
> ation lingers. And the desperation resulting from the alien-
> ation lingers more powerfully. The alienation and the guilt
> linger so long, so hopelessly, so powerfully, that one must
> eventually bury them in a façade of autonomous indiffer-
> ence, bury them in resignation. Guilt and alienation are
> givens, however, that will not be denied. Bury alienation and
> guilt in numbness and after a while one does not notice. So
> Jeremiah says, "Everyone is greedy for unjust gain, they heal
> lightly saying 'Peace, peace', when there is no peace..."[5]

As a result of alienation and guilt, Brueggeman suggests that it is
easier to give into the temptation to bury the pain than it is to face
it. Yet the end result is far more painful. We opt for short-term pleasure when we fail to face our shadows. If numbness and alienation

are acceptable to you, then bury your pain. The deeper you bury your pain, the less alive you will feel, the more agony you will endure, the more alienation you will experience and the more numb you will become.

Refuse to deal with your inner pain long enough, and behind your façade of "I'm just fine" will be despair, agony and misery. But become willing to walk through the valley of your internal shadows, and you will experience the comfort of God in a way that will enlarge your capacity for a more rewarding, fulfilling and abundant life.

There is nothing in my rational mind that wants to face my shadows or pain. Everything at a logical level says to run from the pain and save my life the expense and the cost of additional heartache. Yet it is precisely my running from the pain that guarantees that I am trying to preserve my soul—my ego—from the necessary death that releases me from alienation and separation. If I am disconnected on the inside, I am surely not connected to anyone on the outside.

Divorce yourself from yourself in order to save yourself, and you lose yourself in the process. On the other hand, if you lose your need to control life from the limited view of your ego, you will actually find it taking on a dimension of empowerment you never before knew.

Finding Peace in the Shadows

If you fail to allow the shadows to lead you to a place of surrender and wisdom where you make peace with those disowned parts of your life (particularly the pain you are trying desperately to avoid and make go away), then you are refusing to die to your ego-centered need to be in control. What is the end of all that? You abide alone.[6]

However, if you embrace the journey, go through the valley of the shadow of death and face the pain, then you will begin to bear much fruit. In other words, your outcome changes. What grows out of that soil where you entered into a place of surrender emerges at an entirely new level of life experience. You will feel connected and in a flow that you never before knew.

You may ask, "Well, what if some of the mess I have to face or the pain I have to deal with serves no purpose at all?" Then you simply can discard it. However, you won't know that by running from it, will you? Whether it is purposeful pain or purposeless pain, you cannot know until you face it and deal with it. If you don't deal with your inner pain—mark my words—you will medicate it in some way, form or fashion, and your shadows will become your demons and drive you. You will stop being led.

Shadows of Double-Mindedness

What happens when you do not submit your shadows to the process of the valley of death? Your ability to be powerful will eventually be undermined. Shadows of internal conflict or double-mindedness will emerge, and they will determine whether or not you can move mountains with your faith.

Do you believe that you can really move a mountain? Or are there parts of you that say yes while other parts of you say no? There may be areas lurking in the shadows of your soul that refuse to support you in your endeavors, lying in wait until you take that risk—that all-important leap of faith. Then, at the moment when you need enormous inner strength, they come out of hiding and sabotage your efforts. Are there parts of you that hold to a former and "lesser" identity that make trouble when you are trying to move forward?

Having a Double Soul

Doubt has to do with being at variance with yourself. It results in analysis and hesitation when you ask God for wisdom. Childlike trust is difficult to recapture because your analytical mind finds reasons to criticize the "still small voice" inside of you that invites you to break unhealthy and unproductive behavior patterns and to adopt faith-based responses to the challenges of life.

Doubt disconnects you from faith to such an extent that you fail to receive anything from God at all. That hesitation creates an awful restlessness in every area of your life. Doubt looms large over every decision and every action, creating double-mindedness.

Double-minded people are wind-blown, tossed by circumstances, living in instability because they have failed to apply what they have received when they asked for wisdom.

Questioning the wisdom that has been given, the double-minded are not grounded in their behavior or their beliefs. They create a situation of overload in their souls to the point where they live in two souls. They cannot handle where they are, and they cannot accept what they have been given when they cried out for wisdom. The end result is often depression and pain. The awareness they once sought has now become a horror they want to avoid.

The double-minded cannot walk patiently by faith. This requires trusting for benevolent outcomes. It also requires modeling confidence, which creates growth and transformation. Instead, such individuals move further into the realm of speculation and fantasy, avoiding taking responsibility for the decisions that they make.

This self-deception says, "If I don't make decisions, I am not responsible for the outcomes." In actuality, if you don't make a decision because you can't decide, you have made a decision not to make a decision. Therefore, you receive back in your own person a lack of clarity and confusion. Sometimes the only way to break such cycles is to make a decision and stick to it, even if you are afraid it is not the best decision. When you are in a double-minded state, the enemies of your soul can take advantage of your weakness and drive you farther into the dark hole of despair, keeping you from obtaining the outcomes for which you long.

In the twenty-first century, our addictive need for control is going to cause greater rifts in the human soul. If we fail to seek for wisdom beyond ourselves, borderline personality disorders will not be the only thing on the rise. All kinds of yet unnamed ailments of the soul will be a side effect of the information age and the worldwide web. Some people will find it easier to live in a cyber world and detach from living with real human beings. This will create multitudes of false identities behind which to hide on the information highway—only to reap great barrenness of the soul as a result.

Identity Issues

Many of us are at variance with ourselves because we doubt who we are. The will to accomplish something may indeed be present, yet the know-how to accomplish it may be lacking. Something in us says, "I know I could do this if I only had the tools, but since I don't have the tools, I can't do this." On the one hand we seem to display a high level of confidence, while on the other hand there is a dark shadow that hides our fears and self-doubts until the precise moment when we are ready to make progress. Then doubt shows up like an uninvited guest to trash our party. So we wrestle with an identity issue: *Who am I really?* This question plagues more people than you realize.

I cannot move a mountain if I do not know I am a *mover* of mountains. Disappointments in life have trained me to become a mountain *climber*. All the tools in my tool chest are mountain-climbing tools. All the skills I have developed in my life are mountain-climbing skills. Now I am invited to move mountains instead of climb them. I am invited to work smarter with my faith and not harder. However, I am in conflict. I am in doubt because at my core my identity is climber. I have had to survive by climbing up the rough sides of my mountains. I have adapted and learned to love hard work. I have sweated and strained to get ahead, make a living and carve out a life. That is who I am.

Now, this is not the way I would have wanted to be or would have dreamed I could be. But I have had to learn to love and accept the way things are. So my faith moves in the direction of working hard, expending a great deal of effort and seeing little spurts of growth here and there. Forget quantum leaps of faith. That is an unreal world that I have never seen, tasted, touched, smelled or heard.

I cannot know myself by myself. Someone once said, "It takes two to know one." There exists a humble faith in myself that is an outgrowth of my faith in God once I realize that God knows me. It is not the activity of an inflated ego. The inflated ego believes that the world revolves around it—it counterfeits faith. True faith in God involves the experience of union with God and will bring with it a humble faith in God's ability to move through me—a humble faith in myself.

The ability to move mountains with mere words requires that I give up my preconceived notions as to how the universe works and how reality is created. The presence of deep doubt will confirm my limited worldview. In other words, if deep doubt exists in my heart, not only will the mountains not move, but also doubt will cause me to say, "See, I told you so!" when faith fails and shadows prevail.

Getting Help While Going Through the Valley

Not everyone can recognize when God sends circumstances or people to help guide us through the valley of shadows. While I cannot give you theology for an angel earning his or her wings, I can tell you that the best people to guide us into the future are the ones who have learned from their past mistakes. Their wounds have become our gifts; their pain has become our promise. If you have a hard time getting through the valley of your shadows and tend to want to avoid your pain, ask God, and sooner or later help will come.

God's help, by the way, does not look as we might expect. The messengers He sends sometimes appear weak but are amazingly wise. The old expression "Don't look a gift horse in the mouth" is appropriate here. When we ask God for wisdom in the midst of diverse tests and temptations to doubt and be double-minded, we must not despise the messenger or the way in which God's wisdom shows up at our front door.

Wisdom is not always given in pristine and perfect ways. It comes at times in inscrutable ways, ways beyond figuring out. It often comes disguised in weakness and may even appear to be faltering. It may indeed come by angelic assistance, but more than likely a flesh-and-blood helper will show up. He or she will help guide your feet into the way of peace through the low, dark places where your fears and doubts have been hiding for so long.

Coming Into the Light

Personality disorders lead the field in terms of twenty-first-century maladies. People have been getting close to the "edge" of their flat worlds. Their belief systems have not been adequate or accurate enough to serve them in facing the way things truly are and have left them doubting who they truly are. They feel impotent and powerless to cope with life in the fast lane. They have lost their balance and cannot seem to regain it. Just pick up any newspaper or turn on any newscast, and you will discover that the evidence of psychological imbalance is high.

Can there be true psychological balance apart from the God experience and the communion in the Holy Spirit? Not really, because unless everything is brought to the light, it remains powerfully cloaked in darkness. There in the dark fear and doubt take on an ominous quality and rule in the land of shadows. There where the fear of death reigns supreme we need to become aware that facing our shadows causes them to lose their power and control over us.

Whatever lurks in the shadows has the power to work against us because it stays in the dark, having its effect precisely because we fail to take ownership of it. Whatever is brought to the light becomes light. It is brought out of the shadows and can no longer work against us. So your challenge is to become as open, honest and transparent about the things that you feel, the things you believe you need and the things you want more than anything else, even if you don't believe that having them is possible.

Most of the things you feel—your shadows—are tied to unpleasant memories of events in your personal history. Dumping those "files" is best accomplished by bringing them into the presence of God. This is part of what prayer is all about. It involves speaking to God about your shadows and leaving them with Him. It also involves believing that God is listening and that He cares for you with a love beyond measure and without limitation.

If we ask God to show us how to behave and to believe, we will move beyond our shadows to a new place of healing and wholeness. We will eventually lack nothing if we will be patient in our faith. As faith grows, it will cleanse our souls of the deep doubt that has anchored itself within.

My most formidable opponent is a man named Mohandas K. Gandhi. With him I seem to have very little influence.

—Mohandas K. Gandhi

Chapter 5

Structures of Internal Beliefs

I can recall my first job as a salesman. I worked for a company that sold cutlery, and it was without a doubt the best cutlery on the market—and probably still is to this day. The cutlery was made of surgical steel, and the steak knives cut through metal without getting ruined. The scissors cut a penny in half with no effort at all. We were sold on the product, and it really was a great deal for whoever would buy it. I was convinced it would sell, but I found that every time I was invited to go out after my training period, I would freeze right at the moment when I was supposed to close the deal, and I did not make the sale. I did not want to feel as though I was forcing the prospects to make a decision they did not want to make; however, I never had the guts to ask them if they even wanted to make the decision.

After two weeks of this self-sabotaging behavior, my manager called me to ask why I was not producing. He reminded me of how well I did when I was in training and how much promise I showed for a future in the business. I told him all the surface things that went wrong. I looked at a client's living conditions and decided they just could not afford the cutlery. I looked at their body language and felt they were disinterested. I looked at their facial expressions and assumed they were not convinced.

All of these excuses were my way of projecting onto my leads my own fear of rejection and my own negative perception of traveling salesmen. I had an internal belief, an image of a salesman that I did not want to be like. I did not want to be pushy and obnoxious. I did not want to overstay my welcome, and I did not want to be like the vacuum cleaner salesman who came to our house when I was little, offended my mom and would not take no for an answer. If I peeled back the onion of my internal beliefs, the root issue behind my behaviors was my memory of that vacuum cleaner salesman. I believed that if I were selling something door to door, then I would be just like him. I wanted everybody to like me, even if I didn't make a living, and no one liked the vacuum cleaner salesman.

I never opened up and admitted all that to the manager because I was afraid to be that real, and I probably was not ready to be that honest with myself at that moment. The revelation came in hindsight. Needless to say, I was no longer on the sales force, and it was the last sales job I had for a long time. It was not until I removed the deep doubt about who salesmen were and who I was that the mountain of not being able to sell a worthy product was removed. At my core there was an internal belief that powerfully impacted my ability to succeed as a salesman.

Our belief systems are like layers of an onion, and we need to learn how to peel back each layer in our hearts to get to the core of what we really and truly believe about God, about ourselves, about others and about the world around us. These other beliefs can cause us to have, in addition to our faith and obedience to God, many layers of resistance inside of us. Without realizing it, this resistance causes us to run from mountains when they do not move and to run from truth when God shines a spotlight into our lives.

The Power of Internal Beliefs

Internal beliefs hold enormous power over every facet of our lives, even when we do not realize it. Consider diet methods as an example. Are the methods we employ to change what causes things to work, or is it something else at a much deeper level? For example, does everyone lose weight on the products that are advertised on infomercials or on television commercials? When one diet program has you counting your carbohydrates and another has you eating anything you want, then which one is right, and which one is wrong? Which one will really work? Which one really won't?

Surprisingly, every diet system works. They all have testimonials and high success rates with many individuals. Maybe the issue is not the carbohydrates or the protein as much as it is whether or not you believe that it will work for you. Your belief will determine your success.

If in your heart of hearts you truly believe that what you are doing will work for you (which is a faith issue), more than likely you will see results. Say what you will, but Richard Simmons has won the hearts of millions with his weight-loss program. But is it the discipline, or is it an ingredient in his communication and his empathy that those who follow him buy into?

Jesus spoke to a tree that bore no fruit, and His words caused it to die overnight.[1] Maybe it isn't as absurd as it seems. In recent years I have met a few dear souls who talk to their plants and tell them to grow. I used to think that they were just old and weird—perhaps even losing a grip on reality as their arteries became hard and shut down the supply of oxygen to their brains. Then I read some studies by scientists and horticulturists that said talking to plants had a measurable effect on their ability to thrive. Perhaps all of creation is waiting for us to find out who we really are.[2] Maybe we really do hold the key to setting things free to their greatest potential once we embrace our identities and honor our place in God's economy.

When Peter saw the tree had died, he was amazed at the effect that a few words spoken with the powerful conviction of pure belief had on the world of matter. What kind of energy was contained within those words of his Teacher that had the power to dry up the root system of a tree? Peter was trying to sort it all out. This was so different from how he and the others dealt with disappointment and obstacles that stood in their way.

When Jesus told His students to have faith in God,[3] He was setting the stage for them to come to grips with their real potential. He modeled how to handle disappointment and not shrink back from faith. And now He was acting very subtly as the pace car in the spiritual Indy 500, setting them up for the ride of their lives in the hope of having them catch what He was inviting them to chase after.

Beliefs and Passion

These guys were fishermen. They knew water, boats, nets, pike, bass, perch and maybe a blue gill or two. Their identities were formed by the rugged and challenging world of the ocean. Yet as they observed Jesus, they experienced an awakening of desire deep inside of them to do the same things He did. Was this intentional on His part? You bet it was! It had nothing to do with their education, their social status or their occupations. He was awakening them to the wonderful fact that their present position was not an indication of their future potential in God.

Jesus knew something about them that they did not know about themselves or had long ago forgotten. Buried deep within the soil of their spirits were the seeds of whom they were called to be. Nevertheless, years of setbacks, delays and disappointments had caused their dreams of ever becoming all that God intended to die. They had stopped believing in themselves and in the God inside of them.

As Jesus walked out a greater than human life before them, He was actually revealing how far from truly human their lives had come. Christ understood what His followers could potentially become, and He attempted to be an example for them to follow. In seeing His unique life, they were being awakened to their own unique lives, beyond the bondage of their wrong beliefs and the limits of their doubts.

If Peter began to believe he could move a mountain because his desire was awakened by what he saw the Teacher doing, then all of his behaviors in the stories make sense. He was the impulsive risktaker whom we all admire. If there is one thing that Peter did not do, he did not play it safe—EVER! He lived life on the edge of adventure with all his foibles and follies. He was out there beyond the edge, beyond the flat existence of everyday life after he saw the rich existence of the Nazarene.

"I want some of that" was Peter's motto. Being around Jesus provoked something in Simon Peter and the others and called out of them the desire and ability to do things according to new beliefs that they were beginning to accept about God, about themselves and about the world in which they lived. They began to experience some results because they were set up to believe for success and not for failure.

If I believe that I can speak to mountains and watch them move, then what I believe will cause me to become a mountain mover. I will start behaving as if I am already a mountain mover even if I have never moved a mountain in my life. Awaken in me the desire, the love and the passion to move mountains, and I will believe with all my heart that I can do so. That passion will awaken within me a confidence to start talking to every mountain and every molehill in my path. That passion will set things in motion for the victorious future that I always dreamed about. Maybe every mountain won't move instantly, but I know I will have embarked upon a journey that will ultimately bring me to my desired future.

Your Belief About God

How can I do all that? The answer is simple: by laying hold of faith in God. The power of God is available just for the asking. There are many things that Jesus could have said to Simon Peter about the fig tree and the mountain. But Peter's heart wanted to know the secret to the kind of power he saw demonstrated in the life of his Teacher.

The real underlying issue before any mountain can even be spoken to or moved is your perception of God. How do you see God? What is your belief about God—really? Don't recite a couple of lines that you have pushed to play over and over again. You need to truly understand what your heart believes about God before you can begin to bring the shadows of doubt into the light of truth. How do you relate to God, really? How does your internal belief system cause you to act toward God?

Is God some cosmic sheriff who is keeping track of your violations and writing out citations and summons for you to appear in heaven's court? Have you ever felt that God is out there in the great beyond, far removed from your present circumstances and hard to get a hold of, that in the overall scheme of things you really are not that important?

True confidence in myself rests upon a quiet confidence in God, that He can and will move through me to help me move every mountain in my path. I will never approach God at a level of my experience if in my beliefs I do not expect God to work with me in facing my mountains. Faith is challenging to walk out because, despite my religious upbringing and training, I also have formed beliefs based upon my life experiences. What I believe about my experiences combined with my imagination (whether accurate or not) determines my response to God and to my mountains.

Faith and Action

Sometimes our religious activity is born out of a need to keep ourselves distracted from having to deal with what life has handed us. Most people do not realize how asleep to God they are in their lives, even though they go through all the motions and appearances of devotion. Ask most congregations in America what their minister, priest or rabbi said the previous week, and you will find out just how little most people retain of what they hear. It's not that they are not paying attention. It's that they have heard so much that they can't apply it all. Most of us never apply what we hear to our own experiences. What I hear needs to be grounded in my experience of faith to ignite it into mountain-moving adventures.

I need to mix faith with the input I am getting, and that requires doing something at a practical level in the laboratory of my life. If I do nothing, I will not create a feedback loop to enable me to monitor my own results. *Feedback* is a term originally coined by electronics wizards. The process refers to the return of a portion of the output signal from one stage of a circuit or amplifier to the input of the same or preceding stage. It has come to be used by a new generation of teachers and learners to describe the difference between a desired result and the actual result obtained. In the early

1970s it came to mean the information about the result of a process or experiment. It corresponds to the response you get out of what you put in.

When there is no feedback there is no retention. I have not been able to contain what was given, so I put it out of my mind. You can refresh my memory about it. However, if you give me no prescription for how to live it out, I do not experience any of the benefits of what was said, and I certainly do not have any dynamic encounters with God. God is not known by information; God is known by revelation, and there can be no revelation without experience. It is the experience of God that brings us to the God of the experience. More often than not, I experience God first and understand God afterward.

The Process of Finding Genuine Faith

Jesus modeled lessons about life in God, stimulating His students to act upon the things that He modeled. We need to lay hold of faith, for it is not only fact—faith is action. Faith is realized in the doing. I cannot just stand there—I have to do something.

It is in that crucial place of doing that I discover the blockages that keep me from obtaining the promises for my life. Only as I take the challenge and boldly attempt to put faith into action will I come face to face with my sabotaging beliefs. If I never attempt to walk in faith, I will never find the opportunity to discover my personal roadblocks, my sabotaging beliefs about God.

I am going to make some mistakes, and some of the feedback . that loops its way into my experience will be the opposite of what I had expected. Is that failure? Of course not! I need to give myself permission to make mistakes because that is how I learn and grow.

Too many of us grew up in environments at school and at home in which everything had to be perfect the first time. The final outcome of all those years of learning wasn't geography or algebra, biology or English literature, but rather that we had better get the right answers. I have seen grown men and women, some well advanced in years, sob uncontrollably when I invited them to give themselves permission to make mistakes. I have even seen people get healed of nervous conditions and chronic pains because, for the first time in their lives, they stopped demanding perfection from themselves.

Faith is a learning process. We need to be very careful not to unconsciously demand others to get it right the first time. We can address the issues of where people broke faith. But even at these moments we need to always affirm them and remind them that all of us have had to learn by making mistakes.

Healing for the Inner Man

It is important to recognize the way we have handled disappointment, for every disappointment in life provides a backdrop for the next one you encounter. Life is full of uncertainty and shattered expectations. There are tons of fig trees that are out of season and cannot satisfy our hunger, yet how we respond to those trees is vital to what we set ourselves up for the next time we encounter an illusion. Many things in life offer the promise of something and deliver nothing of what they promised. The fig tree offered a promise that it would satisfy hunger, but in actuality it was an illusion because it could not deliver what it promised.

Our minds need to be healed if our bodies and our lives are going to be healed. Double-mindedness, doubt, uncertainty, despair and all the other things that travel with those companions wage an endless battle in the arena of our inner man to keep us from the victories and empowerment of faith. We need to become healers of the soul and invite others to experience with us the healing presence of God.

The Hearing of Faith

We have come to accept that faith comes by hearing. But do you know that there are different levels of hearing? Having hearing ears is tied to more than what your natural ears hear. Somewhere between your auditory canal and your heart, words of faith pass through filters and layers of memories, imaginations and beliefs that interact with them and find a home your heart. All of this happens so quickly that you are not even aware that it is going on. That's the reason two people can hear the same thing, and one will experience freedom and relief or healing and recovery, and the other person will say that none of it makes any sense.

Everyone processes information differently, and everyone learns differently.

You can hear the statement "have faith in God" entirely differently than someone else. If our desire is for everyone to enjoy the benefits of following the blissful life of real faith, we need to discover how each person is hearing what they are hearing.

Rabbi Breslov made this statement seventeen hundred years after Jesus lived: "You are wherever your thoughts are. Make sure your thoughts are where you want them to be."[4] When Jesus said, "Have faith in God," He was inviting His disciples to a new way of thinking and feeling. He encouraged them to develop new ways of thinking and looking at what was real and what was not real. Christ wanted His followers to understand how important relationships are to God the Father. He invited them to come to a place of childlike and implicit trust and confidence that they were not in this alone, that God Himself was a source of power and a resource from which to draw so that they could live in victory. The source was God, and the resource was faith.

Your heart is the seat of your being. Out of your heart flow the issues of your life. For Jesus, the path to freedom started with the inner man. Cleanse what is going on in the heart first so that everything else in your life will then fall into an appropriate place. When everything inside you fits together the way it is supposed to and is properly aligned, wonderful things happen.

Believing begins in your heart. Your heart holds an awareness of your beliefs, your desires and your dreams. There in that deep place the connection is made to all things seen and unseen. By getting in touch with what you truly believe in your heart, you can release faith as tiny as a mustard seed and can move a mountain.

When the soul is neglected, it doesn't just go away. It appears symptomatically in obsessions, addictions, violence and loss of

When the soul is neglected, it doesn't just go away. It appears symptomatically in obsessions, addictions, violence and loss of meaning.

—THOMAS MOORE

Chapter 6

Sabotaging States of Mind

I am mindful, even at this moment,
I am mindful, even at this moment, of a woman who never fully of a woman who never fully dealt dealt with issues from her childhood, growing up in a home with with issues from her childhood, an alcoholic father and a controlling mother. She saw herself as needing to rescue her dad from her mom. Yet she saw that her mom had to keep it all together, or at least believed she did.

She developed a love-hate relationship with both parents. On the one hand she wanted to protect her dad because she felt he was hurting both from the alcohol and his wife's perfectionism. But she also wanted to have her act together, so she modeled her mom's supposed perfect behavior, which was really an extreme form of control. She grew up physically but remained a child emotionally. At midlife she left everything—home, children and husband—for a fling with an emotionally unstable young man who brought out of her all the things she hid in the dark and denied as a child.

By the way, she was married to a minister, and they were involved in full-time ministry. What legacy will she leave for her children? The same one her parents left for her.

When individuals live out their entire lives trying to be the people they think they ought to be, but never facing who they really are in the mirror of truth, eventually they tend to self-destruct. They end up behaving in ways that leave those who thought they knew them scratching their heads and asking, "Who is this person?"

Many individuals arrive at a crisis point in their lives where the closets they buried their internal baggage in become overcrowded. There comes a moment when someone or something accidentally triggers the closet door to open, and piles of junk come falling out all over the place.

Some ignore the obvious things going on in their relationships, thinking that if they just trust God, everything will work out. With regret I have witnessed over and over that this kind of emotional stuffing eventually explodes into abusive situations and short-lived marriages.

You can hide or try to conceal the symptoms of your pain, anger and wounding, but only temporarily. Eventually all the denial, all the stuffed emotions, all the shame, disappointment and hurt will take a toll. What you have hidden even from yourself will be revealed, and the longer you wait, the greater the accumulated deferred interest to your relationships, your emotions, your mental health and your physical well-being. Dismiss the shadows in your life long enough, and your body will begin to show signs that you are taking a beating. It may be a digestive problem, a circulatory problem, a glandular problem, a hormone problem, a problem in the bones, a problem in the organs or a problem in the immune system. Your body remembers the things you tuck away and try to ignore instead of facing and resolving.

I cannot tell you how many ways my body took the heat over the years because I refused to deal with pent-up issues in my soul. The states I lived in were often states of emergency. I ran on adrenaline, trying to fix everything, making sure that I was doing everything right, only to find that I was wearing myself out and never coming to terms with what was robbing me of the state of peace. My unresolved internal issues denied me the real peace of mind that was my birthright and my inheritance.

Whatever you neglect early in life comes knocking at your door when you grow older. We spend the first half of our lives trying to make it, get ahead, press through, make the grade, make a name for ourselves, find our soul mate, stake our claim, build for our future and get our nest egg. Sadly, we wake up halfway through the journey and find ourselves wrestling with the question: "Why am I doing all this? What is this all about anyway?"

But we do not have to let the toxic debris that fills up our souls bring us to a destructive point of crisis. We can face our painful issues with brutal honestly and let the truth set us free.

You cannot avoid the truth. You will either embrace it in your heart and experience genuine transformation, or you will prove it in your experience. When you refuse the proof of what ageless wisdom has revealed throughout the generations, you will find reproof in your internal wounds and your physical stresses.

Understanding Your States of Mind

From the time you are born until the time you die, you will experience many states of mind. Your state of mind does not merely include your thoughts, but also your feelings, your emotions and even your physical posture. The body is the laboratory in which you work out the challenges of life from the inside out. If your head hangs down and your shoulders droop, you are in a depressed state of mind.

Breeding Hypocrisy From Shadows

Hidden, incongruent shadows are states of mind that have been stuffed into the closets of our souls. These states of mind do eventually surface in our behavior, often at the least opportune moments. These divisions in our hearts can manifest themselves to others as extreme hypocrisy. Even the best of people have knee-jerk reactions to seemingly minor events and blow off steam for less than appropriate reasons.

Has someone you thought had the perfect marriage ever gone through a bitter divorce? Have you ever heard someone say one thing publicly and then find out they were doing something very different privately? Have you known spiritual leaders who disappointed you, even though what they said changed your life? Don't be too quick to condemn them. They are as human as you and I are, merely revealing that they need to reverently engage in working out what God is working in them. Perhaps they feel they do not have what it takes to confront the shadows in their lives, or perhaps they are too afraid or feel they can't ask for help. Instead of them moving their mountains and casting them away, the mountains move them and cast them away.

More than ever we need to give ourselves permission and respect to ask others to help us find our missing pieces. When you do not know which way to go and you have lost your direction, you need to ask. Just make sure you ask someone who has both eyes open.

Escaping Regret

I have seen a number of people die in my brief stay thus far on this planet, and many of them had a deep love for God, for life, for people and for their purpose. Yet they died with regrets in their souls because of things they refused to deal with, face, own or acknowledge. Mountains that could have eventually been moved never were because the individuals did not know how to process their doubts. They lived their lives under the power of their doubts because they did not possess enough confidence to open up and get some assistance in the healing of their souls.

Too many individuals feel they have to keep a stiff upper lip, trying to give the impression that they are really walking by faith when inside they are driven by doubt.

When Truth Comes Knocking

Undetected shadows that are deeply embedded and deeply held in our hearts will eventually show up at our doorstep, knock on the door of our hearts and ask to come in to those places where we have shut out the God of truth. In the Book of Revelation, Jesus Christ said to the church, "Behold, I stand at the door and knock."[1] I find it fascinating that religious people tend to apply these words to those who have no relationship whatsoever with Christ. When spiritual people think that they have arrived and apply what they read to everyone else except themselves, they are in grave danger of missing reality—in fact, they may have already missed it. Yet no one seems to have the guts to tell them.

Preachers have preached dozens and dozens of sermons on "Jesus is knocking at the door of your heart" and applied the sermons to everyone other than those whom the text addressed. How sad that the greatest psychologist who ever lived, the Wonderful Counselor, is ignored by the people who claim to know Him the best. In this text Jesus was knocking at the door of a church where He was being talked about, where programs were going on that were about Him and where people were hearing His words and His teachings, but the church wouldn't let Him in.

It is absolutely crucial to deal with what may be lurking behind the closed doors of my heart where shadows live. The voice of God is the persistent "knocking at the door" that I have refused to open.

Hearing the Knock

The knock of truth can come as feelings or states of emotion that force you to search out the reasons behind these signals from your soul. A sense of restlessness might interrupt your desire to relax. That's a knock. A knock can also come as an interruption to your plans, such as a state of frustration, or it can come as a state of fear when something in your present circumstance triggers a memory of a past experience that you vowed you never wanted to go through again. All of these states of emotion indicate that below the surface lies a hurt that needs to be identified, owned and healed. The knock of truth comes so that you can be led into a way of increasing faith and abundant life.

Keep overriding those knocks, ignoring them, repressing them or dismissing them, and the voice of God will be heard less and less. The power of God will greatly diminish in your life, and you will be left to cope without God's help. You may find that the only things that help are antidepressants, beta blockers, a pacemaker, a by-pass, another piece of cake in the middle of the night or another multilevel opportunity like the three thousand others you already tried to get out of debt.

If you refuse to open the door of your heart to truth, you will probably be tempted to silence the knock of your needy soul through unhealthy behaviors. Addictions, compulsions and obsessions come in all forms, shapes and sizes. You can be very involved spiritually, giving the appearance that you are experiencing God.

But you can still be bound to a sexual addition, a work addiction, a codependent addiction, a drug addiction or any one of a number of other addictions that help you avoid dealing with the painful shadows that control and destroy lives. Consciously you know that these behaviors damage you, but you keep doing them.

According to statistics, more and more of us are taking refuge in unhealthy behaviors. Granted, many people do not have deeply rooted addiction problems, but don't underestimate how widespread the problem is, even in the church world. Many of us struggle greatly to find our lives, and many more of us have lost touch with what is going on inside of our souls.

Many individuals have been out of touch with what is going on inside of them for so long that they live in a numb state of disconnection and don't even realize it. Then something simple like a song or a flower triggers a memory and stirs up hidden pain.

When you hear a song that touches something so deep in your own soul that you cannot hold back the tears, what is going on? Prior to hearing the song your emotional state seemed quite rested and stable. Then the words and music penetrated a deep chamber room in your heart, and a flood of tears came from nowhere. Roberta Flack sang about it in "Killing Me Softly With His Song." Sometimes poetry, art or drama can read your life, opening up locked doors in the hidden places of your heart that you have refused to enter and causing things to surface that you chose to forget were even there.

Connecting With Your Emotions

A popular singer once crooned, "I'm in an awful way." Have you ever felt as if you were in an awful way? I am sure there have been times that you have, and times in which you needed to talk to someone about it yet chose to keep it all to yourself.

Some of us remember times when we were in an awful way and talked to the wrong person. Instead of giving us the support we needed, that person became an instant expert on our problems, on what we were doing wrong and on how our failures and short-comings impacted our situations. They may have even scolded us for our negative confession.

I have heard people quote, "I have not been given a spirit of fear,"[2] while all their behaviors were fear driven, including their confession that they had no fear. Some call this faith, but I believe that it is denial—which is spiritually, psychologically and emotionally unhealthy.

Knowing that I have not been given a spirit of fear does not mean that I still have worked out all the fear issues in my life. Do I need to affirm what I have been given? Absolutely! Do I need to deny what I am wrestling with? No way! I admit it precisely because it no longer has to remain in the dark. My fearless spirit will dissolve it once I bring it out in the open. If I tell myself a lie, I remain caught between what God's truth says about me and what I am actually experiencing at a gut level of my state of mind.

I am all for optimism and faith-filled words, but they need to arise within the soul out of a process that unfolds from a central and core place of strength to be genuine and powerful. I am deeply committed to helping people get around the blockages deep within them because sometimes they just get lost inside themselves and don't know where they are or how to get home. Coming alongside others and entering their world is the key to helping them overcome the obstacles that stand in the way of their success and their dreams.

Doubts can come to us out of the shame that often goes masked within our souls because we are scared to face honestly the parts of us that are less than acceptable. We have learned over the years how to keep up a good front in order to have others think well of us.

I have often wondered about some individuals who tried every-thing to change. They were determined not to make a negative confession, but still saw no tangible results in their life experi-ences. They needed to get in touch with their own hearts.

We do not expect to bump into our doubts in little things even though we do. We tend to think that doubts only affect the big things, like working miracles, opening blind eyes and healing lep-ers. But doubts most often impact the little things of life, such as how to raise our children effectively and how to make sure that the large purchase or investment we are about to make is a wise one.

Living in the truth, free from doubt, is a powerful gift. But the cost of truth often requires a life-changing process. In the next chapter we will take a look at how you as an individual can move beyond uncomfortable states of mind and painful, unhealed inner wounds into the power and liberty of truth—beyond a shadow of a doubt!

Those who cannot remember history are

condemned

Those who cannot remember history are

condemned to repeat it.

—GEORGE SANTAYANA

Chapter 7

Breaking the Power of Agreements

I still have vivid recollections of my
fear of the "spanking machine"
when I started first grade. I began

I still have vivid recollections of my fear of the "spanking machine" when I started first grade. I began my education eagerly, believing that the teachers were nice people who were going to teach us how to learn and grow. After all, wasn't learning supposed to be fun?

Well, Mrs. L. didn't think so. I remember praying one of my first sincere prayers at six years of age on the first day of school. It was kind of an orientation day, and we all were in the lunchroom being "oriented." The first grade teachers were telling us that kindergarten was over. There were no more half days of school; this was the real world, and life was going to get tough. School started at eight in the morning, and we would work until three in the afternoon.

Mrs. L. looked as if she stepped right out of a Bela Lugosi flick. Although I was a just beginning the first grade, I had already had the wits scared out of me by *Dracula* more than once. Mrs. L. had a big nose, bony hands and bony legs. When she would put that bony finger out in front of her face and point it at us, I kept expecting her to wrap a cape around her with the other hand and turn into a vampire.

She was like a drill sergeant barking commands at all of us, commands that were followed by threats. Her threats were underscored with a graphic description of the "spanking machine." This instrument of torture was kept in the dark basement of the school—where only bad children went.

We did not yet know who our teachers would be, and we were not a praying bunch. But we were sure beginning to cry out to God that we would not get Mrs. L. If the devil had a sister, I was sure it was she!

Thankfully I wasn't assigned to Mrs. L's classroom. When I got home, I found out that she had been around a long time. She had been Uncle Danny's teacher when he went to public school, and he was twenty-two—really ancient! Uncle Danny told me that once he had acted up in class, and she beat him up. I felt so grateful to God for delivering me from the jaws of death at six years of age.

It all seems very funny now. But I can assure you that the threatening look of a teacher in the days of corporal punishment and the idea of a spanking machine in the dark corridors of the basement of that old school building did nothing to enhance the enjoyment of the learning experience for this six-year-old. I learned how to be afraid of learning from some of those who invited me to learn.

Even though there never was a spanking machine, I assure you, I believed in it long after I stopped believing in Santa Claus and the Easter Bunny. As long as Mrs. L. was around, and she was around as long as I was in the primary grades, I believed in the spanking machine.

My friends and parents tried to convince me that no spanking machine existed. I refused to believe them. In my heart I deeply believed in that instrument of torture, and I believed that Dracula's wife was in my public school and was the operator of it! I had made a choice—an agreement with my fear. There was no changing my mind.

Forming an Agreement

Other beliefs about your ability to learn, to grow and to change are equally difficult to let go. If you agree with a lie that says you cannot learn, it will be difficult for you to learn. If you form an agreement with a lie that says you cannot change, it will be tough to recognize when you actually do change. Until you believe you can influence your future, you probably won't attempt to move any mountains. You will learn to camp around your fears and set the limits of your existence and your capabilities based on what stands in your way and blocks your vision.

During adolescence, Henry did not believe he had the capability to learn. He agreed with the assessment of his teacher even though he resented it. Inwardly, the authority figure in charge of helping him to learn embedded in him a belief that he was not capable and that he could not learn. Once he agreed with that belief, he made an internal contract with it. It was etched in steel, battleship steel to be specific, and the hull of the ship felt impenetrable.

Henry's performance in math never rose above the level of his belief because he did not know how to cancel the agreement he made. It shaped his behaviors and reactions and pushed other more positive things in his heart farther and farther out of reach. The power of that agreement caused him to live in the shadow of doubt for a very long time.

Breaking the power of agreement takes effort, time and the help of the Holy Spirit to go back and cancel it.

From the time we are young children we tend to unconsciously create our own model of the world in which live. We calibrate all our experiences, store them in our memories and then make our decisions based upon those memories. In this way, we shape our futures based upon our past.

Compensating Behaviors

All learning requires that you be in a place on the inside where you feel worthwhile and capable. Henry, like many of us, did not know how to support his belief that he could, so he grew to believe he could not. In addition, his environment seemed to support the belief that he could not and caused him to fulfill the limiting expectations of others. He spent all his energy trying to cancel an agreement he made with a belief.

Henry did not believe he could stand up to the pressures of the school environment, and at times the home environment, that challenged his "I can." Therefore, he was powerless to move the battleship off his chest. He became entrenched in the "I can't," even though deep within him he wanted to believe the "I can" without a doubt.

In addition, being called stupid created in him feelings that kept recurring for years when he was challenged to learn something new that involved mathematics. That state of mind became a stronghold. It included a thought process, an unpleasant memory, self-talk and negative feelings that held it all together. In that state it was impossible for him to succeed, which led to the development of compensating behaviors.

Some of those compensating behaviors and beliefs created as much unrest as the root belief system and emotional state that was anchored to it. The powers of darkness were able to keep him in the dark for a long time. Like Bill Murray in the movie *Groundhog Day*, he found himself reliving the same event over and over and over again.

Do you have images from your own past, like Henry's, that form a stronghold of insecurity, self-doubt or any other set of debilitating emotions and beliefs? Deliverance requires more than a rebuke to a demonic entity. It involves taking captive a thought system. The walls around that stronghold need to be torn down, which involves removing the deeply embedded pictures, including seeing yourself as inadequate or as a failure. It also involves disconnecting from the emotional venom poisoning your remembrance of the event that was at the root of it all.

Agreements and Self-Talk

Let's take a closer look at the impact that agreements can have. I want to provide you with tools to either move the mountain all at once, or to chip away large chunks of it at a time and use the broken pieces to fill in the gaps in the low places in other parts of your life.

The experience of failure in math created in Henry a belief called "something is wrong with me." That is a very powerful and damaging belief. If you believe there is something wrong with you as it relates to your learning capabilities, then no matter how hard you try, you will never succeed. You are in a battle you cannot win, for you are fighting against yourself.

Take that one isolated area of difficulty in a subject known as math. When you form an agreement with a cruel accusation, as Henry did, it creates self-talk. You now say to yourself, "Something is wrong with me." You have now generalized the whole of your life from the inside out as fatally flawed. You have made an internal agreement and formed a belief that is no longer a specific response to a math challenge. It has become a generalized challenge to your entire existence.

If you happen to have a challenge in algebra or geometry, does it mean you are a stupid person? Does it mean that you do not have what it takes to go to college? Does it mean you will only be average or less than average throughout your entire life? The meaning you attach to your agreements affects so much more than the actual event that generated the faulty belief.

Negative Introspection

If you believe that not only is there something wrong with you, but that you are less than average, then you will start looking inside for the reason that you are less than average. No one ever improved in life by negatively turning in on themselves and searching out their faults and foibles. This kind of negative introspection only drives you deeper into the dark shadows that rob you of the faith to move the mountains in your life.

Are you living with feelings of being less than worthwhile, powerless and maybe even hopeless, even though you put up a tough and strong exterior and appear to be very spiritually active in the pursuit of God?

Agreements and Imagination

How does feeling powerless and believing you are powerless affect your imagination? I guarantee you will see yourself as weak and powerless, and your heart will cooperate and provide a picture to you of just how weak you believe you are. Your imagination is subservient to your beliefs.

Even if you choose to see the possibility of what you could become, if you have formed an agreement with a negative belief about who you could become, your negative belief will win. Your positive image of your future will be undermined by your agreement. You will find some reason to invalidate a picture of yourself succeeding. You will say something like, "Oh, I can see what I would look like, but that will never really happen for me!"

Remember the crowd that died in the wilderness and never made it to the Promised Land? They saw themselves as "grasshoppers" in their own eyes, and they saw the inhabitants of the land as giants by comparison. They saw themselves getting stomped on, and as a result, they died never having to face that possibility. They did not believe they had what it took to get to where they were promised they could go. Even God could not convince them otherwise.

That is how powerful your beliefs, your agreements, your internal contracts are. Have you ever felt the way that they felt about themselves? If you see yourself as a grasshopper and have to go up against giants, you feel belittled and powerless. You cannot be hearing faith in your heart. If you did, your spirit would respond differently.

Perceiving Clearly

Faith comes by hearing,[1] but in order to hear you need to perceive clearly. Your eyes need to see clearly and your heart needs to feel clearly. What did the wilderness wanderers hear when they saw themselves as grasshoppers and their enemies as giants? Did they hear the crunch of their backs being broken as their enemies stepped on them?

It may not seem very significant, but I can assure you it all added to their not being able to live long enough to cross over into the very thing for which they longed. This goes on in those areas in each of us where we struggle with feelings of inadequacy. Who told you that the older you get the less you will be able to learn, change and grow? You are invited by God to be a lifelong learner.

Do you remember the movie *Short Circuit*? Robot Number Five discovered it was "alive." What he craved was "input." For Number

Five, all of life became a learning experience. Although part of your own learning experience might have been painful because you also learned that not everyone was supportive of your existence, learning was still an enjoyable event.

Number Five's love of learning enabled him to translate every situation from setback to feedback. He managed to overcome the things that tried to overcome him because he kept learning and moving to progressive levels of competence. Ironically, he was just a machine, built by a human being. You are fearfully and wonderfully made, and you have the capability of turning every apparent setback into feedback for future success. You were "built" by God to be a lifelong learner.

Experiencing Your Senses

All your senses are involved in the learning process. The desensitizing of your life is what kills your hopes and your dreams. It eats away at you from the inside out. Unless you are in a place internally that is fully alive and well, your learning will be limited and inhibited.

Lepers do not lose their fingers from the leprosy. They lose all their feeling in their hands, feet, fingers and toes. Rats chew off their digits, and the lepers do not feel a thing. As they lie in the streets of many of the impoverished nations where the disease still abounds, they fall asleep and do not know when they are providing a rat its dinner.

If you lose your feelings and become desensitized, you lose your ability to enjoy life to the fullest, and the rats come out at night and eat away at you while you sleep. You need to allow for the experience of all your emotions, even the painful ones, because they are a part of your life. If you experience your emotions, then you can also receive the healing that is behind the pain of your emotions.

Have you discovered some things in your life will not just go away? You need to walk through them. Passing through the valley of shadows brings us out of the power of deep doubt, replacing it with bold confidence.

Breaking the Power of Agreements

It is not enough to recognize how deeply embedded your beliefs and agreements are. You need to have a way to get to the next level. If someone does not give you a way, you will find it harder and harder to believe that you can get there. That is why changing your beliefs is not enough and is not that easy. You can pump yourself up only so long until you cannot motivate yourself any more because you cannot see results.

It is like the old adage: "Give a man a fish and feed him for a day. Teach him how to fish, and he'll feed himself for a lifetime!" It is not enough to believe you can go fishing; someone has to show you how to do it.

We were born with a love for learning. But events can happen along the way that kill our creativity and destroy our love for learning. If you make agreements with limiting beliefs based on someone else's opinion about your capacity for learning, you are reduced to behaving according to those beliefs. Inside you may hate the fact that you have accepted the "I can't do it." Yet you have no one to show you *how you can*. You really *can* if someone will just show you *how*. The place where you are living also affects what you believe about yourself, others and God. Your environment will either support your beliefs or invalidate them.

Finding Deliverance From Inner Pain

The battleship that was supposed to be able to defend and fight back for Henry was sunk by a hit from his teacher's battleship.

Henry's teacher, brother and father formed an alliance, even though they did not realize it, and sunk Henry's battleship.

Henry had already developed a "life's a battle" metaphor while growing up in the inner city. But now he no longer had the ship or the artillery to fight back. Every time he rose up to say, "I can," the battleship pinned him to the bottom of the ocean floor inside him and said, "You aren't going anywhere!"

The presence of the dysfunctional agreement served as a blockade, a roadblock on the path to Henry's dream called "I can." The mountain of self-doubt did not move because he doubted in his heart that it would. The most powerful words of negation in the human soul are "I can't." Those words will stop you every time. Henry had to discover how to pass through that low place and face the shadows that kept him bound to doubt in order to rise again to a new level of confidence.

Breaking Your Agreements

The wound in Henry was emotional, intellectual, psychological and somehow even physiological, as evidenced by his restlessness and drivenness. Healing required examining the "I cans" and the "I can'ts" that existed in Henry's life.

All of us tend to live between the imposed limitations of someone else's false assessment of our lives and our own internal agreements. The only way to break the agreement is to walk back through each phase of it and cancel it out by remembrance, renunciation and release. Consider it in this fashion:

REMEMBER

Remember God and the events that have challenged you.

Remembering God is the act of engaging God in conversation, which is what prayer is all about. It also involves putting God in remembrance and unconditionally surrendering to His healing presence and healing voice. Choose to trust the Holy Spirit to bring you into the process of facing painful memories and erasing the limitations that have held you bound.

What has held you in chains has not included God at all. Bring Him into the process of remembering. In that dialogue of remembering prayer, you need to be real, honest and open—not holding anything back.

You will learn how to open up and let God touch the areas where there has been discomfort and pain. You may need help in order to do this. You may need to seek out a competent and caring individual who walks at a high level of integrity and compassion and is skilled in areas of *spiritual direction*. You need someone who can mirror your emotions and your self-talk to help you see how you are dealing with what is going on inside. Such an individual does not necessarily tell you what to do. He or she actually mirrors what you are doing so that you can discover for yourself where you keep tripping over the same pitfalls.

RENOUNCE

Next *renounce*, verbally and aloud, the agreement you have made within yourself with the limiting beliefs, refusing to allow them to have a place in your life any longer.

Renunciation has to be verbal for a number of reasons. You are dealing with something deeply embedded in your soul. Part of the challenge you face is creating a new pathway for the circuits in your brain to follow. You have told yourself for so long that things are one way. Now you are actually deconstructing the former roadway in your soul on which the negative cargo traveled.

Speaking out that you are no longer in agreement with the negative, false beliefs will put all your senses, both external and internal, on alert. You are taking charge and taking rule over your spirit, your mind and your body.

In addition, you are in a battle with unseen forces, spiritually evil and destructive forces that are bent on your demise. Those entities have devised plots and strategies to undermine your progress and your success. As a child of God, you already have all the resources and power you need inside you to overcome those forces. The God who is in you is greater than all those forces combined.

When you speak out the canceling of those agreements, you let the forces of darkness know you are no longer aligning yourself with their scheme to destroy you. You are no longer walking in the nonaffirming and destructive beliefs that have sabotaged you. You are saying that you are ready for a fight, and this time you are going to win.

The only good fight is the one you win, and you are letting them know that you have taken a faith posture because the faith fight is a good fight.[2] It is the one you always win, no matter how hard the enemies of your soul contend against you.

RELEASE

Finally, *release* your association with the old feelings, memories, hurts, unforgiveness, beliefs, attachments, self-talk and agreements that held you captive.

Release all of it to God, who will totally eliminate it. Realize that anytime you even slightly recall the belief system with all the feelings and vain imaginations associated with it, that it is part of the old you. Today you have stepped into the new you, a person who is totally disassociated from that stronghold.

Release it all, acknowledging that you no longer see yourself the old way, hear yourself talking the old talk or feel yourself responding or acting the old way any longer. Old things are passing away, and new things have begun.[3]

Walking Out the Process of Change

One of the challenges you may face as you begin to break those agreements is that at first you may experience what seems like a burst of progress followed by a prolonged season of failure. In that season of failure you may confront the behaviors, emotions and feelings that you are seeking to overcome. It is all part of the process of becoming whole, and it is necessary for the learning experience.

When you walk by faith, you may fall a few times—maybe even six or seven times, or more. Nevertheless, God will keep picking you up until your mistakes become feedback for your next level of success. You learn things from the walk of faith; the pitfalls along the way are necessary for your growth.

Then in place of that stronghold, you have to learn how to rebuild your frame of reference from something that is of good report, beautiful, pleasant, virtuous and attractive.[4] When you feel that you are struggling, try this:

- In the moments when you are tempted to go back to those feelings and memories, let your mind go there.

- Only this time release your anxious thoughts to God in prayer and wrestle them out of your experience (or continue praying until the feelings and negative thoughts are gone).

- Then watch as the very peace of God becomes the military garrison that surrounds that area of your heart and your mind, keeping out that destructive tendency.

Give God room to work, and you will see a difference, feel a difference and hear things from a different perspective. You will even hear a different voice. Instead of hearing the voice of a nonaffirming teacher (or parent, sibling or so forth), you will cultivate your ear to access the presence and peace of God. You will hear the affirming voice of your heavenly Father, and it will settle like the balm of Gilead on your war-torn battleship of a heart.

Will this really help you? Beyond the shadow of doubt!

Symbols have
the capacity
to touch us
not just on an
intellectual level
but on behavior
and emotional
levels as well.

Symbols have the capacity to touch us not just on an intellectual level but on behavior and emotional levels as well.

—ALBERT EINSTEIN

Chapter 8

The Inner Language of
Images and Symbols

Our thoughts are not necessarily known or fully understood on the conscious level. They are "known" on a level below our conscious awareness. Here is a simple illustration: If you have ever learned how to drive a car with manual or stick shift, you first had to learn all the steps. You operated the clutch, the accelerator and the brake along with the stick shift with one hand, held the steering wheel with the other, and at the same time kept your eyes on the road and managed to drive the car.

I can remember the many moments of panic and disorientation that I put my trainer through as I learned to drive a manual shift. Eventually I got it. No longer did I have to think about all the various tasks that had to be accomplished at the same time.

Driving a stick shift became an unconscious act.

On the other hand, I remember trying to teach my wife how to drive our stick shift Toyota when we were younger. It was a beautiful car, one that I intended to own for a long time. That was until I discovered that she was never going to translate the skill from a conscious level to a subconscious one. The moment of truth arrived during one of our teaching sessions one afternoon while pulling out of a driveway into moderate traffic. The road that she was entering inclined upward in the direction we were headed. She was in reverse and had backed up just fine.

As we backed into the flow of traffic, she could not manage to shift out of reverse into first gear. Cars were moving around us in both lanes as she rolled backwards down the slope. She did not have the presence of mind to put her foot on the brake, and was so preoccupied trying to get out of reverse into first that she failed to notice an eighteen-wheeler proceeding up the hill at a rather quick rate of speed. We were rolling backwards in the direction of the eighteen-wheeler and progressively gaining momentum. She actually didn't even bother to look in her rearview mirror. Her belief system was, "If I don't see it, it will see me."

Given my great propensity to react out of my intense Italian nature, I found that the decibel level of my voice was now loud enough for the whole neighborhood to hear me. My fear was enough for both of us. It did not dawn on me that in a "learning environment" students do not thrive on panic and fear. She already had a bit of her own, and my Italian nature seizing the moment to assist only sent her fears off the charts.

She now froze with panic, which soon turned to mild form of Scandinavian "rage" to match my Italian "fear."

We were only feet from the eighteen-wheeler when I managed to get my leg over the console between the bucket seats and get my foot on the brake (because hers wasn't there). She proceeded to get out of the car in the middle of the street with traffic stopped in both directions and the eighteen-wheeler now stopped inches from our bumper. She left me sitting on the passenger side of the vehicle with my leg straddled over the console, depressing the brake pedal. I was holding on for dear life while I tried to figure out how to get my whole body to the driver's side to get out of the flow of traffic.

Needless to say, it was my wife's last lesson on becoming unconsciously competent at stick-shift driving. When we finally did manage to both get back in the car and I was in the driver's seat, I was strongly encouraged all the way home to go to the car dealers the next morning and trade the "stick shift" vehicle in for one with automatic transmission. The learning process was never complete, and the behaviors never became unconscious for her.

Having said all that, things that happen at a level below your conscious awareness affect the things that you do. This can be both positive and negative, for all behaviors are welcome ones. Consider those who need to inhale smoke and nicotine into their lungs every day without thinking twice about it. This is an activity whose roots go deeper than what the smokers are consciously aware of. If you were to ask a smoker to give you a reason for doing what he does, he might find it difficult, for smoking is never about the cigarettes.

Food addictions are not about food either. Any addiction is a substitute for something emotional that the heart is craving but does not know how to get another way. Cigarettes, food, alcohol or any other addiction symbolizes something to a deep place in the heart and meets an unmet need. Getting in touch with your own symbols and metaphors is part of learning how to deal with your interior life.

The Symbolic Language of the Spirit

At the core of your being, your very essence is spirit. Your spirit touches realms seen and unseen and communicates in a language all its own. It is the real you, the hidden you, the you nobody knows except you and God.

Spirituality requires that there be spirit and Spirit. There can be no spirituality without your spirit and God's Spirit. In addition, spirituality cannot exist without images because the language of our spirit and God's Spirit is a language of images, symbols and metaphors. When we are truly spiritual, we combine spiritual thoughts with spiritual words.[1]

Spiritual thoughts are communicated from the deepest places within us, somewhere down deep in the chamber rooms of the heart. The "innermost parts" of your heart are likened to chamber rooms.[2] In the Hebrew language, innermost part meant a room or a parlor that afforded privacy within a building or house. The "secrets" of the heart[3] are the hidden things at the very center of your spiritual life. In those chamber rooms are your treasures: your hopes and longings, dreams and desires, yearnings and cravings. These treasures are placed there by God; they are designed to shape the course of your life and bring you to your destiny.

Your personal history is shaped under the hand of God and is directed by the Spirit. The Spirit searches the heart of God on your behalf, and your heart and spirit on God's behalf. In addition, it is your spirit, not your conscious mind, that knows your own thoughts. St. Paul makes it evident that there is a difference between what takes place within us at a conscious level in our hearts when he says, "For who among men knows the thoughts of a man except the spirit of the man, which is in him?"[4] Behavioral sciences now acknowledge that there is both a conscious aspect to our nature and an unconscious aspect of our nature.

The Language of Dreams

I am sure you have noticed that at night your dreams have a language all their own. Your dreams are composed of your interior metaphors and symbols based on your waking hours and your history. This is why you cannot go to a self-help section in a bookstore and buy a book of dream symbols. One symbol does not mean the same thing for everybody because everyone is different. You need to learn how your own heart, your own family, your own ethnicity and culture and your own environment have shaped your heart's view of reality, as well as your heart's taste, smell, feel and sound of reality.

If you have a dream about being in a restaurant and having the waiter pass you by, and I have a dream about being in a restaurant and the waiter passes me by, we may not be dreaming about the same thing. We would need to examine what a restaurant means to each of us individually, what a waiter symbolizes to us and what being passed by means. For you it may have something to do with a business deal that went sour the day before. For me it may have something to do with a hunger for attention or love that went unmet in a public context. Dream interpretation is not as easy as some people want to make it. Many tend to oversimplify it, expecting everyone to apply the same meaning for the symbols and metaphors.

You have to know what is going on in your heart to grow and become whole. But you cannot do that alone. It takes two to know one—you cannot know yourself by yourself. You need caring friends and an intimacy with God to help you.

Shadows that lie below the level of conscious awareness that are hurtful or harmful to us need to be brought to the surface and owned and acknowledged. Treasures that God has hidden in us also exist in the chamber rooms of our hearts. These treasure stores are waiting for us to awaken to our potential. At the appropriate time, they need to be brought to the surface and drawn out of us.

Facing Our Challenges of Understanding

As we approach a new millennium, hearts are crying out for more than the fluff of superficial spirituality. We are tired of pat answers and formulas that give only a temporary lift and do not last in our life experience. We face several challenges of understanding. These include:

- Understanding ourselves
- Understanding others around us
- Understanding God
- Making ourselves understood by others
- Knowing how we are understood by God

God approaches us more from a "ancient pathway" that is well worn and proven than from a modern and oversimplified technique that reduces things down to a formula. It is vital to remember that you are a unique soul with patterns and behaviors that have been shaped by your personal history and your senses, both external and internal.

The Shaping Hand of Environment

Your environment has had a definite impact on how you were formed. If you grew up in a one-room apartment with your mom and five siblings, and your dad was not around, it impacted your opportunities and reactions. If you grew up in a home where your dad was a workaholic and was too busy working to give you a hug, it also had an affect on your behavior.

If you grew up not knowing how to get that hug from your dad—and not knowing how to ask for it—you developed unconsciously an internal pathway to help you survive without his hug so you could get on with life. That internal pathway became so deeply embedded in your inner man that years later you may still be substituting bread, cake, sweets and candy for the hugs you never got. You developed a subconscious strategy for getting those unmet needs met. They became so deeply established within you that when you grew up and realized it was time for a change, you lacked the conscious will power to overcome the compulsion that drove you to the fridge for those empty calories. Those calories became internal symbols of the hugs for which you were starving.

If you grew up in an atmosphere where you had to be perfect in every way, where your words, your appearance and your perform-ance before school, friends and family had to be perfect, it affected your beliefs and values. You learned to believe that it was essential never to make a mistake, never to embarrass the family and never to dishonor a family tradition. That tradition may have been born out of compulsive drives to keep up with the Joneses, but it made little difference. That perfectionism shaped your own priorities. You grew up valuing your appearance, performance and reputation. All of these have their place. However, when such things drive you, it is impossible to become whole without first getting healed.

Who You Think You Are

Environment, personal history, relationships and unmet needs help shape the sense of purpose and mission you have about your life. That is what identity is all about. It is what forms who you think you are (even if it isn't whom you were meant to be). These are the things that also affect your spiritual experience, the way you symbolize God and your relationship with Him.

To experience a renewal of your mind and a transformation of your life, you need to become aware of the ways in which God is working on the inside of you to bring you out of the shadows of doubt and into the light of confidence and certainty.

Overcoming Our Own Inner Resistance

Consider for a moment that one purpose for which the Son of God became human was to disclose to us what intimacy with the Father is all about. He came to those who were heirs of that legacy. Yet they could not see, hear or feel anything He was talking about. Their gates of perception were blocked and shut because of religious thinking, pride and prejudice. Yet the masses living under the darkness of that organized religious world were in need of a Shepherd.

They needed healing, and they craved wholeness, but they did not know how to get there. They did not know why they couldn't get there. Their challenge was to overcome their own inner resistance to truth, a resistance that kept them from the freedom they craved.

When Jesus addressed them, He told stories in the form of parables. The purpose of the parables was to connect them to metaphors that would bridge their external world of material things to the internal and spiritual world they needed to access. Remember, Jesus had to overcome their resistance; the tragedy was they did not even know they were resisting. This is the way that the powers of darkness work. They blind our conscious minds to the light of the glory of God, and we are not even aware that we cannot see.

Jesus' heart was deeply moved to heal the masses. But to do that He had to gain access to their hearts. Since the gateway to learning begins with the external senses—sight, sound, taste, touch and smell—it was necessary for Him to come through those gates to touch their inner world. Jesus Himself declared that the reason He taught in parables was because the multitudes had eyes, yet could not see, and had ears, yet could not hear, and had hearts, yet could not feel. [5]

Desensitized by Religion

The religious system of the day had caused them to become desensitized to the experience of real spiritual release. To them God was merely a concept, not a living reality. How do you penetrate the depths of a person's heart if you cannot get through the gate of his or her understanding? You need to find some common ground in the external world that becomes a symbol for spiritual truth and invite the hearer into a story that allows him to grasp the truth behind it.

That's why Christ talked about things in their agricultural world, such as seeds, farmers, vineyards, laborers in vineyard, weddings, mustard trees, sycamore trees, merchant marines, buried treasure, leavened and unleavened bread, lost coins, lost sheep and lost coins.

As a master storyteller, Jesus created a metaphor that invited His hearers into a rich, full sensory experience that enabled them to see themselves in the story. Then the process of awakening would begin. Since their senses were dull, many stories were needed before they lowered their resistance so He could bring them into the healing they craved. These parables would break down the resistance and hardness of heart the religious leaders had erected at the gates of the people's perception through fear and intimidation.

Through the eyes of Jesus, we got a vivid picture and metaphor of how the multitudes really were. They were "distressed and downcast, like sheep without a shepherd."[6] That was how He symbolized them when He saw their spiritual condition.

The religious thieves had already come to steal, kill and destroy. They had taken away the key of knowledge (the experience of God) by desensitizing them to their own ability to be intimate with God. It was a form of exploitation and manipulation in the name of God that kept the masses dependent upon them. The religious leaders used the sacred structure known as the temple, which symbolized access to God, as a place for merchandising and manipulating the people.

Lying, cheating and stealing were common among the religious rulers of the day, and devotion became a black-market religion. If you brought a lamb without a spot or blemish, the best of your flock, for your Passover offering, those who examined the lamb at the sheep gate before letting you enter the temple would pretend to find a blemish. They would then take your lamb and make you buy one from them, one they had taken from another pilgrim earlier. There wasn't anything wrong with your lamb; they merely made money on you twice. This was all done, by the way, in the name of God.

Is it any wonder that Jesus made a scourge of cords and drove out the merchandisers who were buying and selling sacrificial animals in the temple? It became a big business in the hands of a select few religious scoundrels, and the masses were at their mercy. They were driven by their need for acceptance with God with no other way to get to God except through them. When Jesus said He was the "way,"[7] He was not merely being politically incorrect. He was economically threatening the stability of a corrupt system built to exploit the needy.

Corrupt men who paraded as servants of God in the spiritual arena ran the system. Nevertheless, they themselves were governed by principalities and powers bent on destroying anything that would allow the people to experience God's power and intimacy.

Unlocking the Gates of the Soul

If you enslave people long enough, they become desensitized. They no longer see for themselves, hear for themselves or feel for themselves. Eventually they let the system tell them what to see, hear and feel. The gates to their souls become as locked and guarded as Checkpoint Charlie before Russia and the Communists tore down the Berlin Wall.

That's what happened to the Israelites. Jerusalem, which was to be a place of liberation and freedom, became a city of oppression and bondage. The city of peace became a place of killing those who

were sent with messages from God and robbing those who needed
to receive the healing of God's Word.

Entering Through Parables

Parables were a way of getting past these invisible gates without
being noticed. The defenses of those under siege were high, for
they lived under the fear of more oppression. The Pharisees and
the Sanhedrin demonized anyone who did not prophesy the party
line. As far as they were concerned, Jesus was a rebel. He was a
threat to national security. He was a friend of tax collectors and
sinners. He had powers that none of the religious leaders had. He
spoke as one *having authority*; they spoke as those *taking authority*.
There is a world of difference! He was a healer; they were steal-
ers, killers and destroyers.

They came to make people blind and keep them that way. But
Jesus came to make them see with eyes wide open what was really
the truth. He came to remove the covering that was over their eyes
and the blocks that were on their ears to soften the hardness that
had encrusted their hearts and was keeping them from ever feeling deeply again. He came to heal the numbness and ache in their
hearts that spoke much more loudly than their repetitious religious behaviors.

Jesus saw beyond the public self of the masses to the hidden self
that only they were aware of. He saw beyond their blind spots and
into the deep chamber rooms of their hearts. He came to heal,
restore and empower them to become whom they were meant to
be. He still comes to heal, restore and empower.

Jesus Christ sees beyond your public self to the private self that
you do not allow anyone to see. He knows that place where shadows hide in the dark. He also knows what can heal you there as
well. He sees right into that deep part of you, the innermost

chamber rooms of your heart. That's where God has concealed things of destiny, treasures awaiting discovery that can only be accessed when all of your senses are awakened, your personal history is reconciled and all the parts of you are brought out of the shadows into the light.

Symbols of Our Reality

Change is not always easy, is it? Healing is not always as simple as a one-touch deal. Remember the story of the blind man of Bethsaida?[8] Jesus took him by the hand, re-sensitizing him to an experience of the "feel" of God's power and presence by touching him. Then He led him out of the village, which was the environment where his whole trouble began. Jesus then *spit* on the man's eyes (talk about a sensory experience—I wonder what that felt like?) and invited the man to look up.

Have you ever noticed that we often look up when we are trying to remember something or to picture something we are day-dreaming about? Do you find that when you are praying, you often glance upward in some way?

When the man looked up, he saw "men as trees walking."[9] This man symbolized the reality he saw regarding others. Did he see men, or did he really see trees? Light was definitely coming through his corneas and retinas, but his brain was picturing and projecting what his heart was symbolizing as reality.

If you live in the dark long enough, you will create associations or images about what is in the light. You will see those associations and representations even if that is not the way they truly are to be seen. We see what we believe is there, and it is all based on what is projected out of the depths of our hearts onto the more conscious places of our awareness.

There was no lack in the power of Jesus to heal the man. The spittle from His mouth was a way of softening, lubricating and awakening the man's external sensors, making them sensitive to the light. But once the light came in, it revealed what was hidden in the man's heart. The man had to own his symbols before he could get the second touch that caused him to see all things clearly. He had to verbalize those symbols in the presence of the One who was administering the healing for which he longed.

Once he owned that metaphor and symbol, he received the second touch that put it all in perspective and cleared everything up. It is OK to see men metaphorically and symbolically as trees. It's a commonly understood metaphor.

"You shall be like a tree," the psalmist said.[10] Are you literally a tree? Of course not! But the metaphor of a tree helps you to get a handle on your experience of reality. Wounded or whole, people are like trees. The seed of a painful childhood eventually grows into a belief system that produces fruit. That fruit is doubt that hides behind sabotaging emotions and attitudes such as the statement "life is a battle."

The second touch from Christ upon the blind man's eyes integrated the symbol and the metaphor to its appropriate place. Now the blind man became able to see human beings as they truly were.

Before He departed, Jesus gave the man some final instructions, telling him not to go back to the village. In other words, He told him not to return to the environment that caused him to lose his perspective and his accuracy of vision and that caused him to symbolize life without seeing the real meaning behind the metaphor.

When you cannot see, it is the parable that rebuilds your inner world and reconnects the senses to the heart. Only then can you experience the healing touch that integrates those symbols into total life experience.

The awakening of your senses will move you toward seeing

what is lurking in the shadows of your heart and will move you from the rooted pain. Do you recall Henry's symbol of being stuck under the sunken battleship of pain and self-doubt? Getting in touch with your own internal language of images and symbols, as Henry did, can move you from "I can't" to "I can," from powerlessness to empowerment, from despair to hope and faith. Can you get there? Will you see it? Beyond any shadow of a doubt!

Section III

Removing the Blocks and
Lifting the Shadows

Beyond
the
Shadow
of
Doubt

Beyond
the
Shadow
of
Doubt

We cannot heal the mess we have made of the world without undergoing some kind of spiritual healing.

—M. Scott Peck

Chapter 9

Now Comes a Stranger

Sometimes the best way to discover the parables and metaphors of our own lives is by stepping into someone else's story.

The more I read the ancient texts, the more fascinating they become. As literature, the Scriptures have it all. Romance, intrigue, mystery, war, family crisis, the pursuit of destiny, the discovery of meaning, the quest for the supernatural, the struggles and temptations of life, you name it—it's all there. It is a matrix, a womb of images, metaphors, symbols and representations based on real-life individuals whose experiences invite us to be transformed by their journeys.

You may have found yourself walking with Abraham as you waited for God to show up and fulfill His promises to you. You grew older as you waited, feeling more dead than alive; the womb that was to birth the promise in your life was barren. I am not the only one who has felt this way.

Or have you ever found that you had to wrestle to get what was coming to you? You felt as if you spent your whole life grabbing at someone else's heel, having been ripped off by people who exploited you for their own benefit. In the end you were left so weakened and disabled that you had to limp like Jacob into the inheritance you were promised.

Or did you ever have a dream for the future like Joseph? You shared your dream with the people you thought would appreciate it the most, only to find that they resented you for it, sold you out and sent you packing—never wanting to hear from you again. To top it off, they lied about your whereabouts and made up false stories about you. At some point in your journey, when that happened, Joseph's story became your story.

All of these incredible and wonderful stories provide us with a way of processing our pain, healing our wounds and discovering our options on this pathway toward confidence and empowerment. Sometimes the easiest way to solve our own problems is to see life through the eyes of another person. Entering into someone else's story provides a fresh perspective on our own.

I am convinced that it is in you to get beyond the shadows of doubt and move into the empowerment of real and deep, abiding confidence. You feel the urge within you compelling you to go there. You are thirsty for water to refresh the dry ground of doubt. You crave a meal at the banquet table of faith that will move your mountains and clear a path to the future God intended for you. You long to arrive at a place where you can hear the trees clapping their hands and the mountains and the hills breaking forth into shouts of joy on your behalf celebrating your arrival.[1]

I am going to invite you to enter the story of someone who was just like you and me, someone to whom we can all relate. Even though we each have our own unique way of experiencing life, there are common denominators for all of us. After all, at the core we are all from the same seed.

As you step into the shoes of this particular individual, I want you to enter the story as though it were you hearing, seeing, feeling and taking in the events, the circumstances and the challenges that were coming your way. I want this to be an experience where you are no longer reading about someone else's life. Experience this story as if you are the star of the old television series *This Is Your Life.* You are on center stage; you are the star, and all eyes are on you.

So let's begin our living parable at the beach. The evening weather is balmy, and the wind is calm. The water is clear, and the crowds of fishermen are bringing in their boats after a day's haul. Kids are gathered at the fishing boats of their fathers and grandfathers, helping to sort out the fish that are worth taking to market and tossing others back into the ocean. Fires are lit along the beach sites where moms are grilling up some of the fresh catch. A few torches can be seen out in the water where nets are ready to sweep in entire schools of fish that are sleeping just below the surface of the waters.

Now Comes a Stranger

There's been quite a buzz in town lately. A maverick sort of man with long hair and a rough-skinned, camel-haired coat has been preaching that everyone needs to get ready for a time of great change. God is about to show up in the neighborhood. This hairy man, whose name is John, grew up in the desert. He has no family, for his mom and dad were really old when he was born. That was a miracle in itself. All that is left of his parents is the memory of an incredible experience with an angel of the Lord and a promise that John would prepare the hearts of the nation for the coming of the Promised One.

John spent most of his growing up years in the desert eating bugs and honey (the breakfast of champions), and he wasn't all that great at people skills. When you grow up in an isolated place, you have very few people with whom to interact. But in that place of isolation, John developed an ability to discern the Spirit of God—he was being prepared for his mission.

At the appropriate moment he emerged from the desert and stood in the middle of the muddy waters of an important river. Generations earlier, an entire nation emerged out of the isolation of that same wilderness. It too stood in those muddy waters and witnessed a miracle. The water of that river stood up like a wall, and the entire nation crossed over on dry ground.[2] Not far from where John was standing was the heap of stones that was left in the river as a memorial of that miraculous event.

When this great prophet stepped into the flow of the river, he also stepped into the sacred memory of another hairy man named Elijah. Just before Elijah disappeared from the earth, he had taken off his camel-haired coat, smacked the surface of those muddy waters and made them part once more. Afterward, he walked across with his apprentice on dry ground, back into the wilderness, never to be seen again.

In that same spirit of Elijah, John the Baptist shows up on the scene. His passion is so great, his message so compelling that the entire countryside comes to hear him speak. You come to hear him, too.

A Call of Change

As a fisherman, you are doing your best to keep the family business going while building your future on the past that has been entrusted to you by your parents. John's words touch a deep core inside you.

"Prepare for the arrival of the One whom you have been waiting for!"

Something is about to change, and you feel it in your spirit. Your heart is burning, and you have butterflies in your stomach. What do you do? John is telling you that you need to get wet! So there you go; you walk into that same flow where your ancestors crossed over from a dry place into a high place, where Elijah worked a miracle many years before you were born.

You look at the mound of stones out in the water, and then you look at John as you approach him. He grabs you and immerses you under the flow of that powerful, historic water that will awaken your thirst and hunger for destiny. In a moment of power, something is anchored and riveted to your soul like the iron bar that is bolted to the large wooden gate leading into the Holy City. When you come out of that water, you are drenched with expectation and anticipation.

Somebody is coming, and something is about to change—and something is taking place in you. Things you have wondered about, longed for and questioned are about to be explained in a way that you never thought possible.

Like a metal key being pulled toward a powerful magnet, you are feeling the pull of your future in ways you never felt before. You go back to the beach where you have your life carved out for you, and your heart just does not seem satisfied with the fishing business anymore. You are doing all the same things you have always done. But they do not have the appeal they used to have. When you got wet in the water of the Jordan River, your appetite was whetted for more of what you had never known before.

You have a difficult time keeping your mind on your job because of a yearning deep inside. Your identity as a fisherman, this key from your past, cannot unlock the door to your future.

The pull of destiny is attracting you in ways beyond your understanding, and you sense that something is about to change.

A Promise Fulfilled

It is early in the morning, and there is a stir at the far end of the beach. Kids run circles around a crowd of people who are clinging to a Man, carrying a little boy in His arms, who has just arrived from across the hillside. When the Man had touched this crippled boy, his crooked legs straightened out and he walked perfectly. Now the little boy didn't want to be put down by the Man who straightened his legs. He wanted to hang on to see where the Man would take him next.

The stranger approaches the boat where you are busy cleaning your nets from last night's catch. His voice travels through the air as He speaks with the crowd around Him. It is a calm voice, yet powerful, strong and assuring. It has a ring of authority, but it is so peaceful that it settles like a soothing balm over the torn places in your heart.

You cannot explain it, but somehow you know that the whole reason He is walking on the beach is not just for the crowds. He is coming toward you. What was awakened in your heart when you were immersed in the flow of John's message has caused Him to want to get to know you. He hears the cry of your heart even though you have never spoken of it aloud.

How does He hear that? Suddenly He is standing there at the shore. Your feet touch the water as you pull clumps of tangled seaweed out of your net while at the same time focusing your eyes on this Man's stature and presence. It isn't so much what He looks like that is having an impact on you. It is what you are feeling. You have never felt this way before. He is touching something very deep inside you, and for a moment it is a bit uncomfortable

because it feels as if He can look right through you to see everything that nobody knows about. Still, He gives you a sense that you
are totally and unconditionally accepted in His presence.

He Calls You by Name

The silence breaks, and He says, "You are Simon!" At His words
you feel as if you are about to lose your breath, drop the net and
fall into the water. But you manage to maintain your composure.
You are not going to ask how He knows your name or how He
got your address. It is all a bit much to take in at the moment, but
something inside you says, "Whatever He asks me, I'll say yes!"

When He called your name, you felt an enormous sense of
power. Now you feel as if He knows you inside and out. You are
unnerved, but not fearful; you are filled with awe, not with anxiety.

"You are Simon"—the voice keeps playing in your head at fast
speeds while He is standing there toe to toe with you. He sees you
and knows you. He seems to know where you have been, how you
got to where you are and why you behave as you do. He also sees
where you want to be.

You got wet with a dream of destiny when you were immersed
under the flow of your national history. That water reconnected you
with where you came from. You are a child of Abraham, a *Hebrew*,
which literally means "one who crosses over a river." You have
owned a part of you that had been disowned. It wasn't your fault;
it has been more than four hundred years since a prophet has challenged your people to come back to their place of intimacy with
God. There has been a lot of water under the bridge since then.

Somehow you now are awake to the fact that, just like the river
Jordan, there is a flow to the history of your people, and you are
a part of that flow. What affects one affects all. In that river you are
one with them, and they are one with you. Once you enter that

flow, you cannot leave it the same as when you went in. Now it is too late for you to turn back; you got your feet wet. You are about to enter deep waters, deeper than your feet, your knees, your hips or your chest.

You have just met the Man who is going to take you out so deep that you will not be able to touch bottom. And somehow you know in your heart of hearts that it is what you have been waiting for from the time you were a child. Nevertheless, you haven't been able to put it into words. You could not match words and feelings with the symbols and pictures that were coming from deep inside you. Suddenly, you realize in His presence that the missing piece you have been waiting for is about to be given.

"You are Simon." His words fire off in your brain once more like a gunshot. The crack resonates in every chamber room of your heart. This is who you are, the sum total of what your parents have named you. You were named after one of the twelve sons of Jacob, Simeon, a son of Leah, the unloved wife who felt left out of destiny and cried out to God. God heard that cry and gave Leah a son whose name means "I have been heard."

That's you. Your sense of identity has been waiting for an affirmation that somebody greater than mom or dad, grandma and granddad, greater even than the prophets, knows who you are and has heard your cry. Your whole life has been a cry to be heard, a cry to be understood, a cry to be acknowledged and recognized. God has heard your cry!

Very little actual time has passed as you stand with your mouth gaping in the presence of the Man on the beach. Your mouth tells it all, for it seems as though it's difficult for you to ever really keep it closed anyway. For the first time in your life your mouth is open, and you can't say a thing. He has you exactly where He wants you.

It has not yet dawned on you that He also knows more about you than you know about yourself. You aren't quite ready for that revelation, but in time you will be. When you arrive at that place, all the fears that have been hiding in the shadows and all the doubts that have been getting in the way will be removed.

What you hear next is totally unexpected. Not only does He know where you have been, but He also articulates where you would love to go but have been afraid to admit even to yourself. You don't want to disappoint your dad and leave the family business, but ever since John's meeting at the river, you have been agitated and troubled, just like the waters of the Jordan. You are uneasy about remaining chained to your past. Something in you is crying out for the adventure of a lifetime. You want to find out what you can become. You want to understand how you were built, why you have all these urges, why you see things as you do and why you are never satisfied. You want to be understood, and you want to understand others. You want to connect with people at a deeper level, but you feel you cannot. It's an "I can't" that is getting in the way of your future.

Follow Me

Then He says, "Follow Me, and I will make you someone who can connect with and catch others." He is reading the secrets of your heart. In a few words He touches the stuff that is locked up in the chamber rooms of your heart. He got to the core of your longings without even finding out how you learned to fish or how many kids you had or what it was like growing up. He got beyond the gates of your defenses, circumvented your blind spot, maneuvered around your hidden spot and your shadows and went straight to the secret chamber rooms of your heart. He went directly to that most sacred place inside you that you have kept under lock and key. This tender place cannot be entrusted into the hands of any man or woman. But He has opened the door without even asking you for the key. How did He do that?

Once the Man read the secrets of your heart, what was left but to surrender everything to Him and follow Him wherever He might take you? Talk about power—just a few of His words were more powerful than the endless diatribes of others.

In a moment you realize that He can take you from where you are and give you the skills and capabilities you need to get to where you dream about going. In so doing, He provides the missing pieces. You will arrive!

At that moment you drop everything you have been holding onto and follow Him with empty hands. What a journey awaits you! You are leaving, at least for a little while, everything you have relied on for your existence, everything you have become familiar with, everything you thought you were supposed to be, do and have. You are learning how to walk all over again.

By starting with little steps first and then progressing to bigger steps, you will become what your name suggests: a faith walker! For since your name means "God has heard," then faith is the natural outgrowth. Faith comes by *hearing,* and *hearing* by the word of God.[3]

Now, every time the Man says, "He that has ears to *hear,*"[4] you will recognize that He is calling your name!

An old church spiritual says, "Hush, hush. Somebody's callin' my name!" The most powerful gift you can give to anyone is to call him by his name. When you call people by name, you honor who they are, where they have been and what they are becoming.

Walking by Faith

You are walking by faith to a place you have never been. You are not scared, though; you are excited! So what if the fish don't fill the nets tomorrow? You will be doing another kind of fishing that is worth walking away from all you know.

Some of your family call you back to the nets. They tell you that you are foolish, that you need to come back and be reasonable, that you have lost your senses. You realize, however, that you have actually just gotten all your senses back.

Once you stepped in the river—got in that flow—your history met your destiny. You began to see, hear and feel things that had been buried so deeply that you thought they no longer existed. Your family believes that you are losing everything you worked hard all your life to gain and that they worked hard all their life to give you. But something in you tells you that you haven't lost much. Your destiny is not comprised of these things.

No one behind you can take you to where you are going. These people represent a person that once was boxed in and destined to become what they all expected. Now this Man represents where you are going, and He has the keys to get you there. He will open doors for you that no man can shut and shut doors that no man can open.[5]

Following this Man is costing you a job, a reputation and a social position. But it really does not bother you. It costs a whole lot, but it is worth the price. A sense of joy stirs within. You see that same joy in the stranger, and you want what He has to offer. You have come this far and will not turn back.

You see something else in Him. There is no shadow of turning, He is changeless, and He seems to have arrived at a place that you have only dreamed about. He has no doubts or internal struggles. He will realize all His objectives. When you are around Him, you feel such a deep, abiding confidence that you tell yourself over and over, "I want some of that. I want more of that. I want all of that.

"I want what He has beyond any shadow of a doubt!"

Forfeit your sense of awe, let your conceit diminish your reverence and the universe becomes a market place.

Forfeit your sense of awe, let your conceit diminish your reverence and the universe becomes a market place.

—Rabbi Abraham Heshcel

Chapter 10

Learning to Walk on Water

You are traveling on a pathway that leads to deep confidence by inviting the Spirit of God to integrate all of the hidden parts that are hidden in the shadows of your heart. Let Him lead you to the place where you are reconciled not only to God, but also to yourself. As you do, expect to discover the power to raise you out of the dead things that hold you back from your destiny.

Now that you are walking in Simon's shoes, your heart may be beginning to stir with longings, feeling and desires that have always been there but have not found previous expression. As you progress, pay close attention to your feelings and your self-talk, for they will reveal where you are and even where you have been. In so doing you will become aware of those areas where God is inviting you to grow. Your mind will be renewed as you permit the process through which the Spirit is leading you.

Simon had a vague sense of what he wanted in life. But until we experience the healing presence of God, our destinies are not always evident. If we feel His presence, we enter a place of possibility and access a level of resources that were not available to us until that moment. When Simon was apprehended by the unexpected, loving and disarming call of Jesus, he was able for the first time in his life to act in faith and move toward his dreams.

Let's step back into his shoes now and continue this journey toward freedom from the shadow of doubt and to the power of deep confidence.

Seeing With New Eyes

Word spreads quickly about this miracle worker, and the crowds grow from town to town and city to city in the region of Galilee. You never dreamed that one day you would need to learn the art of crowd control. Everyone seems to press against the Man, and there is little room for Him to breathe.

You also discover something else. You have not seen it before because you were so preoccupied with just surviving that you didn't have time, or more accurately didn't take time, to notice. Everywhere you follow Him you notice people in pain, people with unfinished business, people with issues that need closure and people with illnesses that have afflicted them for years. It is too much to take in all at once.

You grew up with some of these people. In His presence they begin to reveal struggles and pains that you never knew they were suffering. It is disconcerting to hear the struggles of people whom you thought you knew. Not only that, some of these people that you knew as sick all their lives are suddenly well and walking, taking on risks and challenges of those who are half their age. You can barely believe your eyes, for their youth seems to be renewed.

When blind eyes open, it isn't just a shock to the blind. The power that is exercised by that Man shocks you as well, for He has invited you to walk with Him in that same power.

You witness all the pain and suffering that has been around you all your life, but that you have been too preoccupied to notice. We all experience a certain degree of blindness. Some of us are blinder than others, but all of us are in need of a touch upon our eyes. The more you see, the more you realize how little you have seen. You realize that you live your life choosing to see what you want, conveniently blocking out what you do not want to see.

You begin to see that you have built an inner world all your own that is far different from the real world where struggle, pain and challenge exist. Your way of coping with pain has been to escape from it. You realize how many escape routes you have created in your imagination and in your patterns of behavior. These behaviors are as much a ritual as going to the temple to pray, and you hold them just as sacred in your heart.

You begin to realize how predictable your life has become, how much you have taken for granted and how seldom your senses have awakened. You never paid attention to the sparrows until He spoke of them. You were much too busy to consider lilies until He gave you an invitation. After all, weren't sparrows a dime a dozen, and didn't lilies grow in every open field?

At His words you discover that these small living things beautify your existence. They are gifts as well as lessons. If His eye is on the sparrow, then how much more is He keeping His eye on you? And oh, those eyes, the penetrating gaze and fiery passion you feel every time you into them. You can't look into them for too long, though. It's too much to take. You aren't used to the deep awareness and unconditional acceptance that you feel. It seems a bit safer in the dark.

Others keep their eyes on you because they don't trust you. But He watches you because He takes pleasure in you. Being around Him makes you feel that you have great worth. Nevertheless, it's still a bit unnerving. Better not let Him get too close, for He may see things you do not want Him to see, and then what?

Now you begin to awaken to the degree of doubt you have harbored about the goodness and love of God. Your self-talk sounds a little bit like this: "He is definitely too good to be true. There has to be a catch here somewhere. Yes, He's wonderful, but there is something up His sleeve. Yes, He loves me, but there is a catch in this thing. Yes, He says He cares, but just wait until I blow it. You'll see. He's just like everybody else, and He'll be done with me in a heartbeat.

"I'll enjoy the ride while it lasts, because nothing really good ever lasts forever. It's just that I am having too good a time right now to think about it too much. I am sure a day will come when I'll have to face those dragons, but not today. Today there are miracles taking place all around me."

Touching Them, Touching You

You are as much an observer of the Man as you are a participant with the multitudes. You watch Him cast evil spirits out of a woman in the synagogue. When He addresses her root issues, you become aware that you have struggled with the same temptations. When you get away from the crowd and nobody can see you, you secretly ask Him to help you pray through this unresolved area of your life.

Everything He says and does for the people is also for you. Just when you think you have figured Him out and have heard all the truth He has to share, He introduces His most powerful sermon yet. His insights into the human experience touch a cord so deep that you realize He is taking you through a process. Although He is not talking directly to you, everything He says is about you. He touches your pain, your struggles and your frustrations. Never did anyone ever speak as He speaks to you.

Your ears are hearing at a deeper level than ever before, and you discover how deaf you really have been. You are starting to hear the pain in people's voices behind the words they speak. Their words have not changed, but you are hearing them from a much deeper place inside you. You are starting to notice fear in some people's voices, even if they are trying to hide it from you. You are also starting to hear the sorrow in someone's voice that he or she is attempting to mask. You even detect anger in someone's voice when he is working hard to conceal it.

Not only are you seeing what you have failed to see and feeling what you refused to feel, but now your whole being is waking up when you are around Him. Never has He demanded that you see things His way. He is always meeting you where you are, celebrating what you have learned and honoring where you have been. Yet all the while, you are growing by leaps and bounds. He takes time to walk alongside you to give you a new perspective on the challenges of life and the pressures of temptation.

You can't seem to be around Him enough. Every fiber of His being vibrates with the energy of heaven, and when you are close, you feel as though you are touching heaven itself.

He is quick to let you know when He doesn't agree with you. Yet He does it in such a way that you do not struggle to hear it. When you rehearse for Him how others have corrected you, He laughs and invites you to keep moving forward. After a while, because you keep pace with Him, He tells you things that others saw about you that you couldn't see. He causes you to agree with His assessment and to laugh at yourself. You discover that wise people make knowledge acceptable, for that is how He allows you to experience those areas of your life that are tough to talk about.

Things are going along quite well. The crowds are growing, and the sick are being brought on cots and stretchers. The paralytics and the lame are laid at His feet, and the blind are led from every town and village. Everyone that He touches is healed. Never have you encountered anyone with this kind of power or stamina, so touchable, so accessible, so real and genuine, so human.

You feel embarrassed to even be around Him because He is so far beyond anything you could ever be. Yet He keeps including you in the experience. You lay your hands on blind people, and their eyes open. You command evil spirits, and they come out of the tormented souls of the multitudes.

Touching the Lepers

You face your fears, your prejudice and your cultural upbringing. At first you resist, but then you touch a leper, and he is cleansed. Your upbringing taught you that you would become unclean with his disease. But he became clean with your health. You gave him the gift of life. You walk away scratching your head, wondering how you did it. Perhaps you just needed to be willing to touch him. Perhaps the real issue was overcoming your judgment, thinking of him as less than yourself. Once you faced your own internal resistance and overcame it, a touch from you was enough to heal him. Beyond that, you discovered when you touched him that he was just like you.

Lepers feel all the things that you feel and see all the things you see. Perhaps they see even more because their pain has forced them to see what you have willfully spent your life not seeing. It's a tough lesson about love to learn, but you needed to learn it. How can you love God whom you can't see, while you hate your brother or sister that you do see?[1]

Word comes that the Master's cousin John has been beheaded in Herod's court. It is a tough blow to Him. His face reflects the grief and agony of His heart. He doesn't hide it. He grieves openly. That is a tough thing to deal with, watching your new leader process His pain in front of you.

He does try to get away to a lonely place for a while without you. But the crowds won't leave Him alone. They follow Him as you take Him to a lonely place. You arrive, only to find that the people have run on foot over the mountains and through the hills to get there ahead of you.

They want a touch from Him; they have no idea about the pain and grief He is carrying. They do not even seem to care that the sword has now beheaded John, whom they celebrated only a short time ago. It is a shocking eyeopener to realize that the multitudes have forgotten about John and what he meant to them so quickly. If it weren't for him, they would not be prepared for this present moment. It is as if they do not even care about John, much less about Jesus needing time to grieve. The fickle people care only about themselves.

You have a tough time with this. You see how much He pours out, and you want to protect Him from being taken advantage of because you have been around the block a few times. You know that people always take advantage of well-meaning people. That's why it is important to know when to say no and not to feel compassion for everybody. You feel a need to adjust His perception on this one; He hasn't grown up the way you have.

But in His grief He looks at them with compassion. He feels their pain. He suffers with them. He understands that their wounds are so deep that they cannot think about anyone else's pain because they are too preoccupied with their own. They are driven and are not led. They are sheep without a shepherd. When there isn't a shepherd to lead the sheep, a hireling will drive them. These are driven people, so deeply oppressed and distressed that they do not know what it is like to have their needs met so that they can be led.

The People Are Hungry

It is really late in the day, and you and the others approach Him with a problem. The place is desolate and isolated. There is no place for them to go, and there is nothing to eat. It seems important for Him to send everyone home so that they can get home and eat. Therefore you are a little put out when He says, "Feed them."

Feed them? you think to yourself. With what? We haven't eaten a bite all day ourselves. It's been a long day. You're tired. The rest are tired. Feed them? Please! But something in you knows that He means business, and you can't seem to find it in your heart to let Him down. You want Him to think the best of you, don't you? So you and the rest set out to see what food is available in the crowd.

Philip comes running back all excited about a little kid with five small barley loaves and two fish the size of sardines. You want to chide Philip for even thinking this is going to help, but he goes right ahead and gives the boy's lunch to Jesus.

Just when you think you have seen it all, He takes the five loaves and two fish and lifts them up to the sky while thousands on that hillside watch Him. He gives thanks to God for what was given. Then He calls you and the rest over and instructs you to get everyone to sit in groups of fifties and hundreds. You cannot believe you are doing this. You are going through all this for what, to disappoint the expectations of a hungry multitude? *Just watch, you say to yourself, in a moment they'll see who gets the fish and the loaves, and they'll turn into an angry mob for being left out. This meal isn't going feed the first three people in the first group of fifty. Or is it?*

You are a take-charge person anyway, and so you report back that all the folk are seated and ready. Then He does the unimaginable. He calls the twelve of you and gives you each a broken little piece of bread and fish. Then He sends you into a group with them and says, "Just do what I did; break off a piece of what you have, and give it to the first person, and then the next, and so on."

You want to say, "Nothing from nothing leaves nothing," but you know better than to be disrespectful even though you are tempted. You bite your tongue and do what the Man says.

You aren't ready for what happens next. As you break off a piece of bread to give to the first person in your first group of fifty, the bread grows back in your hand. You try doing it with the fish, and the same thing happens. Not only that, some of the folk ask for seconds and you oblige, and it just keeps on coming.

This is beyond belief—you literally cannot believe this is happening even though it is happening before your eyes. You are astonished, amazed, bewildered and confused, but you are having fun in the midst of it all. By the time you and the others finish going through the crowd, everyone has more than enough to eat.

That isn't the end of it, either. Jesus sends you back out, each with a basket to gather up all the fragments that are left. By the time all twelve of you go through the crowd, you are huffing and puffing as you climb the hillside, trying to carry the weight of the large baskets overflowing with loaves and fish.

A Ghost on the Waters

He puts you all in the boat and says He'll dismiss the multitudes by Himself. After a day like this, nothing surprises you anymore. He directs you to go over to Bethsaida to prepare the town for a camp meeting. In the meantime, He goes back up the mountain to pray and seek His Father.

Halfway across the water you are exhausted, needing sleep and trying to process everything that happened. To top it off, the boat is being tossed by fierce winds. You started this boat ride at dusk, and now it is about three in the morning; you should have been in Bethsaida hours ago. This has not been a good trip at all. You and the rest are straining at the oars but can't make any progress.

Somewhere between three and six in the morning, when you are totally exhausted, the Master defies the laws of physics and stands atop the unstable chaos that is resisting you. He walks on the water as if it were dry land.

That's a new twist. You aren't skilled in quantum mechanics so as to come up with an equation that would help figure this one out. This defies every bit of logic in the human brain. This can't be happening—a man walking on water—can it?

With one voice you all begin to scream, "It's a ghost!"

Since you can't explain what you see, you project your images of fear onto it in order to categorize it in your memory. One catch, ghosts can't talk. The moment you scream, this voice that is so familiar to you calls back and says, "Take courage; it is I. Don't be afraid."

Suddenly you leap to your feet and call back through the pounding wind, "Lord, if it really is You, then command me to walk on water just like You, and I'll do it!"

Wouldn't you know it, He responds to you in the affirmative and says, "All right! Come on!"

You are definitely out of your mind—at least your friends think so. They watch you lift your right leg out of the stern of the ship and step down into the water and then follow with your left leg. Lo and behold, you are actually standing on the chaos, and you aren't sinking.

You quickly remember while you stand there amazed that your request was to be where He was, walking on the water. So that is where you are headed. It is the same place you were headed when He met you the first time on the beach and invited you to follow Him. You want to be where He is. Your heart, imperfect and questioning as it is, still yearns for the thing that He awakened in you at the first. You want what the Man has.

Your eyes are riveted to His, and you are doing well. Then you think that the wind has suddenly become visible. Now, you know that you cannot see wind any more than you can see ghosts, but YOU see the wind! Whatever you see that is beyond the level of normal sight, whatever you have projected from your memory that is now getting in the way of your destiny, is enough to cause you to begin to sink into the chaos.

Sinking and beginning to sink are two different things. You watch yourself in slow motion be swallowed up by the waves because you were overcome by the wind. The thing you couldn't see got in the way of what you wanted to see.

You have enough presence of mind to call out for help. He is still yards away from you, but the moment you call you feel the grip of His strong hand clutching you and lifting you up once again atop the chaotic waters.

He is once again alongside you inviting you to walk. He walks in the direction of the ship instead of away from it. His first intention was to pass it by because He expected you to get to where He sent you before He did. Since you missed the lesson, He invites you to learn it again later in a different way.

He Hears Your Cry

Throughout the day your shadows of doubt have hardened your heart. You gained no insight from the loaves and the fishes, and so you failed to access the next level of learning. He intended to pass you by to show you where you could have been. Yet in spite of all that, your cry got His attention. You, Simon, were *heard*, above the wind and the beating of the waves. He *heard* your cry. Don't you just love Him because He *heard* your cry?

The angry waves of chaos did not have the power to silence your cry in His ears. He hears the cries of those who desire to walk by faith, even if they do not always gain insight from their previous lessons. Even when your heart is hardened because of the projections of your past and the casting of your shadows onto your present, He still is willing to walk with you and work with you until you are perfected in faith.

You take a moment to catch your breath because you were hyperventilating and anticipating your death in the chaos. You walk back with Him to the boat, with Him keeping pace with your faith steps showing you how it is done. Then He lets you get back in the boat first. When the rest see that it really is Him, they decide to let Him in the boat.

They still weren't sure at first; you had to convince them. You had to get out of the boat for them to let Him into the boat. You were born to lead. Somebody is following you somewhere, and you are shaping someone else's future with every step you take. It may be a friend, a neighbor, a child, a parent, a relative, an army or a business, but you are shaping the future in spite of your doubts.

You are someone else's key to letting Him in his or her means of transport across the chaos of his or her life experience. By the way, you realize how you disappointed Him by not trusting Him during the day, judging His actions and His motives and questioning His wisdom. You still haven't realized how deep those judgments go. You have one or two more lessons to learn before you really know what it is to face the shadow inside you and overcome the doubt that it creates.

There is one more thing that is important for you to remember. The moment He got into the boat, He bridged the gap. By His grace He made up the difference, and you saw that you were already on the other side without having to row anymore. Once you recognized Him and made room for Him, you were there without any effort at all—beyond the shadow of doubt!

I will give
you the
keys of the
kingdom

I will give you the keys of the kingdom of heaven.

—MATTHEW 16:19

Chapter 11

Keys to the Kingdom
Within You

Three years have come and gone, and you have walked with the Master through a number of very challenging places. Threats from those in authority have brought great fear into your heart. Some religious leaders are seeking to kill the Man who stirred up your secret longings and rebirthed your dream.

It's been three years, but it seems like yesterday. Every once in a while He speaks about sufferings that He will endure, but you brush it off as mystical speech. He always seems to say things with a double meaning. You have come a long way from where you were. You remember when you really thought He was telling people to pluck their eyes out if they had a propensity for allowing their eyes to wander where they shouldn't go. You even considered cutting off the hand of one of the Twelve when you saw him secretly take money out of the moneybag. But the Master let you know with His eyes that He was more aware of what Judas was doing than you were.

That bothers you, too. He seems to allow Judas to get away with theft and continues to let him hold the moneybag. You, John and even James know what is going on. Between your impulsiveness and their raging tempers, you want to fix Judas so he can't steal any longer. You bring up the stealing to the Master when no one else is around except the three of you. After all, money is money, and the campaigns need to be financed and mouths fed. All of you left your occupations and have families to take care of.

When He answers you, it is always something like, "Simon, have you ever lacked since you have walked with Me?" What stings even more, "Has your family ever lacked because you have walked with Me?" What can you say? You know there has not been a moment when your family's needs have been overlooked. In all of those times—and yes, there were some lean times—just as with the loaves and fishes you never lacked, and you never suffered hunger. Something was always left over for the less fortunate. You have to admit that in spite of how much Judas is dipping into the till, there is abundance. It is amazing actually.

Walking With the Master

A lot has taken place in three years. It seems as though you have been in a cram course in spiritual life. You have been more places than you ever have been in your whole life. You have touched more people than you ever dreamed possible, and you have seen more folks than your parents and grandparents combined ever saw in their lifetime.

You are on the "inside" of this new movement. Every time you go back home, family and friends gather around you to hear stories of blind eyes opening, deaf ears being unstopped, cripples walking, lepers being cleansed and dead people being raised back to life. You are a celebrity. You have influence. You have become quite popular with the masses. They recognize you as having been with the Man.

You have also endured scowls from religious leaders who don't like Him as well. But you are a scrapper, and you can defend yourself. There's still enough of the neighborhood kid left in you that you are not going to be pushed around. People look at you with adoring eyes and think you are someone special. It feels really good. You like the attention.

Before you met the Man, the only people who paid you any attention were those from whom you demanded attention. All eyes are on you now. You are the guy who walked on water with the Master. Boy, did that story get out quick. Even the kids in the neighborhood call you "Uncle Simon" now.

People used to be scared of your tough-guy image. But now you are the hometown hero. It is really interesting to you how different your hometown treats you compared to how His hometown treats Him. They celebrate you at home, while they hate Him in Nazareth. Something bothers you about that, and you can't seem to figure it out. In your hometown they see you as "one of us"; in His hometown they see Him as "none of us."

Somewhere in the back of your mind you have these latent fears that the same thing could happen to you someday. But right now you are a star, and everybody, including you, loves it. And the fact that people listen to what you say feels incredible and powerful.

Every so often, when the others aren't around and you are alone with Him, He cautions you about allowing power go to your head. He warns you about the danger of an inflated ego, and you brush it off as inconsequential. You tell Him not to worry, that you have it all under control. As a matter of fact, you let Him know that since He came into your life you are more assured and confident now than you have ever been before.

You have studied His gestures, His mannerisms and His voice inflections so often—and oh, those gazing eyes—that you can read Him pretty well. Every time you brush off His comments and try to reassure Him, you see a pained look in His eyes that feels very disconcerting. You notice it, but you push it out of your mind, not valuing it as an important communication. After all, He still tells you how much He values you and loves you for who you are, and you still have a lot of laughs together. You tell yourself, *He'll see that He's overly concerned about me.*

"You Are the Christ"

It is the winter season, and you are traveling north to Caesarea Philippi to await the arrival of spring and the New Year. Passover is only three short months away. For the past three years Passover has been a time for great campaigns in the Holy City, and you are looking forward to what will happen this year. This Passover promises to be bigger and better than any so far.

He is walking way up north—you have actually never walked this far north with Him before. He stops at a gorgeous spot under a waterfall by a beautiful mountain range. Surveying the surrounding lansdscape, He stands on a huge rock where the waterfall, which is now behind Him, cascades down beyond Him to the hillside below and empties from a ravine into a stream flowing toward Samaria.

"Who do men say that the Son of Man is?" You find yourself, as always, wanting to be the first to answer because being right is important to you. Gaining approval is a need you have had all your life. Now you have found the One who can give you approval, and you want all you can get.

"Some say that You are Elijah because of the way You work miracles," you reply.

John pipes up and says, "Your eloquence causes people to think You are the prophet Isaiah come back from the dead!"

James laughs and says, "Yeah, and You know that silly superstition that has been held by so many that Jeremiah was going to come back from the dead? Some say You are Jeremiah because of the way You actually enter into the grief and pain of the people You touch!"

Then Matthew replies, "Talk about the dead coming back to life, some say You are John the Baptist and that Herod is in a heap of trouble!"

Everyone takes a turn, except Judas who stares blankly and seems disinterested. He never seems to enter into the conversation, and when he does, all he talks about is politics. He is interested in forming a new political party that will usher in a golden era of prosperity, so spiritual things don't mean much to him. He always looks as though he is always planning something, and he is always somewhere else, never present to the moment. Not you though. If something is going on, you are right there in the middle of it all.

"Who do you say that I am?"

Now He is seeking to get something out of you and the rest that is much more personal. It is one thing to consider what everyone else thinks about Him. But since you are up close and personal, He asks how you see Him. You are taken aback by the question. You unconsciously pull back your shoulders and stiffen your body, shifting as you move away from the question.

Once again, in almost milliseconds your memory races back three years and you relive key events in which He spoke while moving in dynamic miracle-working power. A still, small voice from somewhere inside of you that you couldn't quite pinpoint kept saying things like, "This is the One who wrestled with Jacob at the ford of the Jabbok River." You remember hearing, "This is the One who walked in the fire with the three Hebrew boys in Babylon." You even recall that voice saying, "This is the One that Isaiah saw high and lifted up in the temple after Uzziah died." And you recall clearly one event when He spoke of the heavenly kingdom. That elusive voice said, "This is the One like the Son of Man whom Daniel saw in his vision receiving a kingdom from the Ancient of Days!"

It seems as though you have been gone somewhere in your memory for weeks, but it's only been a moment. When you come back to the present, your hands are clammy and your heart pounding a mile a minute. You are now aware that you are seeing Him for who He really is. Jumping to your feet, you blurt out at the top of your lungs, "You are the Anointed One, the Son of the living God!"

Wow, you said it. Those words came out of you from somewhere deep inside. You have never articulated anything like that before in your life! You have just identified Him for who He is to you. You have called Him "Master" before, and you have called Him "Rabbi." Out of respect and dignity, you have even called Him "Lord." But until now you have never called Him "the Anointed One," "the Christ," "the Messiah," "Shiloh!"

This is the One whose right it is to rule. You see Him not merely in the natural. Beyond the olive complexion of His skin, the dark hairs of His long beard and the locks of His long hair, you see beyond what is in front of your eyes.

There is an energetic stillness in the air all around you. You are tingling from head to toe, and you can feel the power surge through you from the crown of your head all the way to your feet. You have never felt so alive in all of your life.

"You Are Simon"

What happens next is nothing short of amazing, exquisite and incredible. The Man, the Christ, the Messiah looks you straight in the eyes and says, "You are blessed, Simon son of John!"

He pronounces a blessing on who you are, acknowledging you not only as Simon, but also acknowledging where you came from. He speaks of you in terms of your dad's heritage, whose name is John. You realize that He sees who you have been up until this point in your life. You are aware in that moment that all things are naked and bare before Him, but you aren't afraid. You are relieved.

Then you hear Him say, "Flesh and blood did not reveal this to you, but My Father who is in heaven."[1]

Whoa, you breathe deeply, pulling your head back as you take it all in. That obscure voice that you heard from somewhere inside was the voice of the Almighty. Imagine that! The God of Abraham, Isaac and Jacob, the Eternal One, the Transcendent One, is talking to you! How can that be? You thought He only talked to the high priest or to prophets. But you heard from the Man Himself, the Son of God, that His Father was talking to you.

God the Father hears you and talks to you! It was God the Father who awakened you when you got dipped in the flow of Jordan's history. He was the silent director and coordinator of the events who orchestrated the encounter on the beach that day with His Son. You are floored. Not only does the Man know you, but His Father knows you, too. He knows your name and your daddy's name!

This is all a bit overwhelming, and you feel as if you are about to fall over backward, just as on that first day at the beach. However, you know that if you fall this time the rock you are standing on will hurt your head. So you take it all in standing on your feet.

All this is happening in split-second timing. Yet it feels as if everything is moving in slow motion, and you are in a place you have never been before. All of a sudden, like the sound of a thousand stringed instruments playing in harmony behind the cascading waterfall standing behind the Man embellishing His words, He speaks again.

"And I also say unto you also, that you are *Peter*, and upon this ROCK I will build My called-out company, and the gates of hell will not be able to withstand your advance."[2]

You are about to fall over backward one more time. It all seems beyond your ability to process. You are feeling many things, and somehow your heart is taking it all in. Yet your mind is totally unfruitful because His words reach past your natural intellect and comprehension. Deep inside you there is the ring of truth about it all. He has just opened up the most unknown part of you that neither you nor anyone else has ever seen, heard, felt or touched. He has accessed the treasure that was hidden in the darkness. It was set there by predetermined purpose of the Father from before the foundation of the world. He just spoke to the part of you that did not come from your mom or dad or your lineage or heritage. He spoke to that part of you that partakes of the nature of God Himself.

He affirmed that part of you that was born neither of flesh and blood, nor by the will of man, but rather by the will and creative Word of God. He just renamed you. You are becoming aware that the longings you felt when you came up out of the water needed affirmation from the One who put them there.

When you emerged from the water it was as though a part of you died. Nothing felt the same after that moment. You no longer felt joy for the fishing business. Everything felt different from the inside out. Things that you used to do no longer appealed to you. Instead, you discovered a new hunger and thirst inside you for things unseen and a passion for life in a new dimension. No one in your total life experience could have brought that out of you.

Finding the Missing Piece

Then suddenly, this Man showed up at the beach and you felt as if a missing piece to the puzzle had been given. A doorway that had been obscured from your inner vision became visible. A chamber room in your heart needed to be opened, but you did not know how to open it. All the keys you had used previously no longer fit. You didn't know where to look for a new key to unlock that one door. That door did not have an iron lock on it; it had a golden one.

Like a child opening a long-awaited gift, you would have loved to peek into that one door in the inner parlor room of your deep heart. Sadly, you could not, for even you didn't have the key. No one in your present or your past had the key either. What good is a door to the secret parlor room of your heart with a golden lock if you have no key?

You had been given all the keys to the other chamber rooms of your heart from your family through your personal history, your environment and your heredity. But no one in your past could give you this key because it didn't belong to you, Simon. You didn't have the necessary resources to access what was in this room.

Simon, in order for you to possess this key, you would have to undergo a transformation at a deep level. In so doing, you would then emerge from hiding in the shadows below the layers of doubt and uncertainty. Somewhere between that door with the golden lock and the necessary transformation lie the valley of shadows and the gates of another realm that held sway over your life because of your fear of death.

A Call for a Larger Identity

The Master speaks, "Simon, for all the light that has come into your life in the last three years, you are still in the dark. You have yet to realize all that My Father has put within you. My Father has heard your cry because you were with Me from the beginning. You were known before you knew yourself. Just as Jacob of old, before he went through the valley of shadows, did not discover who he truly was!

"Your name reveals only one aspect of your nature. In addition, it is only your flesh and blood nature, that part of you with a deep need to be seen, heard, felt, understood, recognized, approved of, appreciated, celebrated and welcomed. But that nature is marred and scarred by many pains, wounds, hurts and scabs. That nature has learned how to fend for itself, act on its own and become self-centered. It is not whom you were meant to be.

"A caterpillar might desire to climb the heights of a tree after spending a lifetime crawling low to the ground, avoiding being stepped on by larger animals, eaten by birds and crushed by unsuspecting human beings. In the same way, when you come to the end of yourself, you will begin to feel the urge to transcend what you have been and what you have known. So, like the caterpillar, you begin to slowly shift your position from one of crawling to climbing. You still move slowly, but you progress toward your desired objective. You know that there is nothing else for you to experience in the crawling life and the creeping life. You need to take on the behaviors of climbing life.

"Some have tried to convince you that you would be crawling all of your life. They have tried to hold you back from the climb you have been making these past three years. Nevertheless, the urge within you—which didn't originate with you but with My Father—has caused you to press beyond the dead things that once were alive for you. You have had to press beyond the skeptics who thought you crazy and beyond the critics who didn't think you had what it takes.

"However, you have pressed and will continue to press. You aren't now where you will be, but you are getting close. Signs of the old life still come through loud and clear when you are least aware of it. Your climbing has merely taken you out of the environment that limited you and caused you to realize that you are capable of so much more.

"You still filter things through your caterpillar senses. There remains the you that needs to undergo the transformation. Leaving an environment that limits you is not enough. Realizing the effects of negative influences and beliefs is not enough. Acknowledging that things were not what they were supposed to be growing up isn't enough. Being around the power of the Spirit and the flow of the miraculous isn't enough. You are still only Simon, the one who always *needs* to know that you are *seen, felt, appreciated and celebrated*. All of which is appropriate in its place. But it is not enough to carry you to the place where you truly long to go."

A Silent Call

The Master continues, "At night when you dream, you see yourself mounting up on eagle's wings and soaring far above the dark clouds that block out the light of the sun. Yet you awaken in the morning to find yourself still crawling along at a slow pace, close to the dust of the ground and unable to mount up because you don't have wings to fly, or do you?

"Was it all just a dream, Simon? Or is it an urge, a divine urge? From where is the dream to fly coming? Even though that door with the golden lock cannot be opened, the call of what is behind that door is seeping through the cracks, just like the water that trickled out from under the threshold of the door in Ezekiel's vision of the river.

"It seeps out from behind the door and talks to you in your sleep. Your dreams are awakening in you something from behind that door with the golden lock. It seeps out in moments of quiet reflection and contemplation when you rest from the battles that seek to steal your hopes away. In those moments, the elusive, still, small and nearly imperceptible voice that has been speaking to you from behind that door hints at your future.

"The Father has heard you, but what you will become remains unclear. Too much of your old life continues to govern your thinking, feeling, doing and speaking. That's the reason My eyes trouble you when I gaze at you at unsuspecting moments. You reveal who you really are when you are oblivious to what you are doing and saying. You want to experience what is behind that door with the golden lock, but you haven't got the key. Well, a moment is coming—and you will know when it arrives—when I will give you the keys to open that door and many others."

The Kingdom Within

"Haven't you heard Me say that the kingdom of heaven is within you? Hasn't it dawned on you that if you have seen Me, then you have actually seen My Father, and you have been seen and heard by Him?

"I will give you the keys. But for now, you need to make room in your mind and heart for a new identity. You are Peter, a very large, living stone. And just like this stone that we are both standing on, you and I will stand together. I will be the cornerstone of the new temple I am building, a temple not made with hands. One made of living stones, those who have seen that they are more than flesh and blood because they have seen Me for who I am.

"In the same way that you saw beyond the door of My earthly identity to what was going on behind the world in front of your eyes, I will allow others to see who they are beyond the veil of their natural identities. I will allow them to peer into that secret place within their deep heart where their new identity hides locked away until the moment they see and affirm Me for who I truly am.

"Simon, until you saw Me for who I truly am, I was not allowed to show you who you truly are. You are a large living stone. Together you and I and the rest whose eyes are opened will kick in the gates of hell, pass through the valley of shadows, obtain the keys of the kingdom and unlock the doors with the golden locks.

"For now, savor the experience that you have just experienced. You are a large living stone, and that is your new identity. Remember who you have been so you can remember that I have purified you from this place. You need to pass through a few more things before your climb is complete and the caterpillar exerts its final bit of strength to survive. Nevertheless, you will get to a place where you will be given the keys! Beyond the shadow of doubt!"

If you have faith as a mustard seed, you shall say to this mountain, "Move from here to there," and it shall move; and nothing shall be impossible to you.

—Matthew 17:20

Chapter 12

Walls of Resistance

Part of experiencing a story is being in it. Granted, we have taken liberty in presupposing your experience of being in Simon Peter's shoes—or sandals if you prefer. But by being placed into a living parable, your heart engages the event in the same way you experience the unfolding of the story line in a movie.

Just like being in a movie, you identify with the main character in a very unique way. Your heart either relates to or distances itself from certain felt needs or responses taking place within the story. As you have read through these last few chapters, you have been doing the same thing. I want you to be aware of what is coming up for you as you continue walking in this living parable.

What feelings and thoughts emerged from your own heart as

you entered into Simon's experience? Truth can cause our spirits to leap. But some aspects of truth can seem too close, shining light into what is hiding in the shadows of our souls and triggering our resistance. If your heart reacts with resistance, it may indicate that you are putting up a wall because you are not ready to face what your heart knows is there.

If that is the case, ask yourself what you are afraid of discovering. Perfect love drives away all fear. But until we trust that unconditional love is leading us to wholeness and freedom, we can continue to erect walls to feel safe. I encourage you to find out what is behind your fear so that you can begin to truly experience the freedom, happiness and hope that is yours as a gift of grace. Do not let fear get in the way of your future.

Every part of you affects every other part of you. When you have struggles embracing truth in one area of your life, every other area feels the impact of that resistance. Ignoring the emotional shadows that you need to deal with will eventually influence your health. To ignore what needs to be dealt with in a particular relationship will eventually influence all of your relationships.

Even though it is painful to face the unbecoming parts of you, pushing emotions back into the shadows creates problems at an unconscious level. You cannot become what you want to be by moving in the opposite direction of where you need to go. If you are not in the process of "becoming," then you are in the process of "unbecoming." What is held at the deepest levels of your being determines your behavior. The deeper the shadows, the more your frame of reference, values and even your physiology are changed.

Judging Intentions

The fact that Simon had good intentions is not in question. However, you know the old adage: "The road to hell is paved with good intentions." I am sure that at some level even Judas had what he considered were good intentions for what he chose to do. Simon judged himself by his intentions. When everything went really well, he took the credit.

Evaluating Progress

Jesus wanted Simon to evaluate his journey and measure his progress based on the outcomes he was getting. That is what it means when He said, "You will know them by their fruits."[1] Our intentions are not the best measuring stick of who we are. It is the outcomes that we get that test our inner person.

The intent of your communication is the outcome you get back. For example, the husband who in a moment of weakness has an affair without thinking does not necessarily intend to make his wife feel rejected. Nevertheless, the outcome he gets is exactly that. His intentions are not the issue. When we have not faced what is lurking in the shadows, our intentions are fuzzy. Our outcomes reveal what is really inside of our hearts—that is the fruit.

Beyond the Constraints of Human Nature

Every human heart longs to find integration between its lower nature and higher nature. Our consciousness was split when the man and woman were expelled from Eden. The guilt of that fall into sin split us, and since then we have been unable to get beyond the natural realm, no matter how hard we try. Without a way through that valley, there is no path to your true and intended destiny.

Many try to dress up the lower nature, creating careful facades to hide what is really inside. Haven't you heard about great leaders who are esteemed for work with the poor but are embezzlers?

What about the person who gives his entire life to educate youth to say no to drugs, but is secretly a cocaine addict?

We were made in the image of God, and our hearts long for that image. Fallen we may be, disconnected though we are, the dream nevertheless remains locked up within us. The signature of God remains affixed to the bottom of the scarred and marred, burned and charred picture of our former selves. The person we were created to be before the Fall of mankind into sin remains deeply held within the memory banks of our souls.

A while back, a famous, century-old Italian painting that hung in the hallway of a state government building was burned completely in a fire. After the fire department extinguished the blaze and cleared away the debris, a clean-up crew came in to pick up the pieces. Much was destroyed.

The painting, so large it covered the entire length of one wall, was charred beyond recognition—except for a small section in the lower right hand corner of the work of art. Upon closer examination, workers discovered that the place where the famous Italian artist had signed his name was preserved. The fragment of the artwork containing the signature became even more valuable after the fire because it was now an even rarer find.

It does not matter that our lives have left us marred and scarred, for the signature of the Artist is still evident in our hearts. We are worth more than we can imagine because of that divine inscription. In addition, the highest price possible has been paid for us to make it through the valley of the shadows.

Simon Peter and the Valley of Shadows

It can be somewhat disorienting to move out from the boundaries of your life's "I can'ts." Get close enough to your roadblocks, barriers and mountains, and they may trigger your deep-seated fears and doubts. We are about to meet Simon Peter at the place where he is going to pass through the valley of the shadows. Like you, I don't enjoy passing through places where shadows are all I can see. I want everything brought into the light, but in order to live in the light, I have to venture into the darkness. You do, too.

Nevertheless, we are not alone when we are in the dark. God is there with us even when we cannot see Him. He stands there within reach, and we are never out of His sight, even the times when we wish we were.

Think of the rod and staff that David spoke of.[2] The comfort we find in these images is determined by what they touch in us when we cannot see where we are going. There is the touch of the rod that directs us toward destiny, as it did for Moses and the Israelites. Moses pointed his rod toward the Promised Land as he stretched it out over the Red Sea. We receive comfort in the staff that is a part of our history, for we leaned on it as our sole visible means of support all the way through the wilderness.

Somewhere between our destiny and our history lies the present pathway where we learn and relearn behaviors and skills. This leaning process takes us to the place of transformation where our lives will prove what is good, acceptable and perfect.[3] It is between history and destiny that we are on the proving ground.

Let's step back into our living parable, back into Simon's sandals to get a better understanding of our own destinies.

Lazarus Is Dead

It is getting close to Passover week, and just as you expect, He does the impossible, topping all of His previous displays of spiritual power.

One of the Master's dearest friends from Bethany has taken ill while you are busy with a campaign in another city. Martha and

Mary have sent word that their brother, Lazarus, is sick, but the Man has chosen to delay His journey to His friend's bedside. He doesn't seem concerned, so you stay where you are.

Besides, you have been receiving death threats from messengers of the Sanhedrin. These religious leaders are plotting to kill the Him. You have never had the jitters like this before. Word seems to come from every corridor telling you that the high priest has prophesied the Master's death. You and a few others are attempting to maintain crowd control for the feast in Jerusalem and keep watch in case someone tries to sneak through the crowd and put a sword through His body.

Four days have come and gone since the news about Lazarus reached His ears. You have just heard Him invite you again for a walk. This time you are traveling to Bethany, the village where Lazarus is deathly ill. You think about the various occasions at the house of Martha, Mary and Lazarus. They always went out of their way to make Him and you feel at home. It was a safe place to just relax and be free from the pressure of the crowds. The moment you walked on their property, angels seemed to guard you from the cares of the world and the pain and suffering that always seem too close.

He would often go up on the roof with Lazarus to talk. Lazarus was outside of your circle. Jesus' relationship with Lazarus was different from His relationship with you. With you He was always dealing with your progress and your unfinished business. Lazarus provided Him with a relationship that was based purely on enjoyment without the need to bring out of Him any great apostolic sense of mission. He always appeared refreshed after spending an hour or so on the roof with Lazarus.

As you walk, you take mental notes because you are now fully aware of the pressures of the life of a servant, always on call, never an hour to call your own. Something in you realizes that there has to be more to life than always "talking shop." You need moments of rest, refreshing and relaxation with people whose life experience and work is totally different from your own. It keeps you rounded and balanced, and it keeps your feet on the ground while your head is up in the heavenlies somewhere.

For Him, as awesome as He is, He also lives close to common folk. There is no pretense in Him. One minute He opens the eyes of the blind, and the next minute He laughs at a joke. You have also watched Him weep over a beggar man at a city gate with lame feet. Sometimes He wept, yet performed no miracle—and you often wondered what it all meant.

By the time you arrive in Bethany, Lazarus is dead. He said that His friend was asleep, but everyone knew that the man was dead. He has been dead for four days.

The Awakening

After both Mary and Martha have a lengthy time of interaction with Jesus, they lead Him to the cave where Lazarus was buried. The body, dead four days, is already deteriorating. You all realize that. He tells you to roll the stone away. You are shocked at the command, but He asks, and you can't refuse.

You help to push the stone far enough from the entrance to the cave that the air outside is able to rush in and push out the stale air. The stench from that dark place is horrific. The air isn't just stale; it is dead! No one can raise a man from the dead after four days. Even the Jewish exorcists say that a man's spirit hovers over his body for only three days. Lazarus has already departed for the place of the dead. His body is rotting, and the worms are on the way.

Power Over What Is Dead

His voice sounds like a mighty peal of thunder when He cries out,

"Lazarus, come forth." Your heart trembles at the sound of His voice. You have heard Him preach, teach, sing, worship and even command evil spirits. But you have never heard or felt the power in His voice that you hear and feel when He commands this dead man to come out of the tomb. When Lazarus, bound hand and foot with grave clothes, comes hobbling out into the light, onlookers scream; some of the professional mourners faint. Martha and Mary stand watching in shock and delight with tears streaming down their cheeks. You can't hold back your emotions. You weep from a very deep place, so deep in fact that you don't know where your tears are coming from.

Word of the incident quickly gets back to the rulers in the holy city, and now it is beyond question; they are going to kill Him. They fear losing control over their seats of power and position with the people. Jesus represents a threat to the status quo.

You remember His rebuke right after that incredible affirmation that your new name was Peter. He was telling you and the others that He was on His way to Jerusalem and would suffer and die. You lapsed right back into your former caterpillar nature and said that you would not have such talk coming from your fearless leader. That was not going to happen because you would not let it!

He looked into your eyes and told the adversary, Satan himself, to get behind Him. The cold, icy chill that went down your spine left it stamped in your memory. One moment you are blessed and promised keys to unlock doors, and the next you are in the hands of the evil one.

The threat of death is now much more real to you than it was three months ago up on that rock by the cascading water in Caesarea Philippi. Lately, you wake each morning with an eerie sense of fore-boding. You are wrestling with feelings that are coming to the surface that you cannot control, but you decide to push them back down because everyone thinks you have everything under control.

One minute you were promised keys, and the next minute the

discussion of death caused you to instantly react. You didn't realize it, but your reaction arose from the fear of death buried deep in the shadows of your soul. It wasn't Him you wanted to protect; it was you! That is too difficult to admit to yourself, so you reject such thoughts.

Your feelings of self-doubt are wrong, and you resolve to prove it. You are going to be the best you have ever been for Him. Your behavior is going to be topnotch; He will not be able to find anything unbecoming in you. You will prove that you have what it takes, even if you have to fight to the death side by side with Him against your enemies.

Back From the Dead

Lazarus has some interesting stories to tell since he came back to life. It is as if he has inside information. He and Jesus pass words and comments between themselves at the dinner table each night during that Passover week that shakes you to the core. It was tough enough handling your encounter with Moses and Elijah on the Mount of Transfiguration. Your fear got in the way there too, and you blurted out some suggestion while under that cloud of glory about building some tents.

The voice that was so appealing as it spoke softly inside you to reveal that the Man you walked with was the Messiah thundered and bellowed from heaven about "hearing" His Son. It certainly was a wake-up call. It occurs to you that it isn't enough to know that He hears you. It is vital that you hear Him, and when you hear Him you need to also guard your heart so it does not shut Him out.

Entering the Gates of the City

As the week of Passover approaches, He commissions you to go into a village and untie a colt that has never been ridden. You bring it to Him, and He mounts it and enters the gates of the city.

The cries of the multitudes are like the sound of many waters. They are reciting the Hallel, the most treasured and celebrated passage in the Psalms regarding the arrival of Messiah at the gates of the city. Waving palm branches and blessing Him, the crowd acts as if it isn't unusual to see Him as the Prince of Peace.

They quote passages and sing songs that apply only to the Messiah. You know that this is making the religious leaders increasingly angry. Sure enough, they demand that He tell the multitudes to stop shouting that He is Messiah.

He replies, "If they don't cry out, the rocks will!"

You wish He had not said that, for it just makes things worse. In a moment when He could have smoothed things over, He stirs them up even more. There is no figuring Him out. You question the wisdom of His actions, but never verbalize your thoughts. You don't want to appear unbecoming.

Early in the morning the next day He wakes you up and again invites you and the rest to walk back to the city of David. He has a sense of urgency about Him. You jump up out of bed, knowing He means business, still rubbing your eyes as you squint from the morning sun. On the dusty trail from Bethany to Jerusalem, you notice a lone fig tree with large green leaves. How strange—all the other fig trees are not in bloom because it isn't the season for figs.

Seeing the tree at a distance, the Master wants to see if there are any figs on it because He is hungry. He heads straight for the fig tree, lifts up one of the large green leaves and finds nothing underneath it. He stands back and loudly and clearly speaks to the tree, saying, "May no one ever eat fruit from you again!"

You note the spot where the fig tree is standing. He is disappointed that there is nothing to eat on a tree that promised to meet His desire for food. When you arrive at the temple in Jerusalem, you have a feeling that He is not a happy camper.

He begins to condemn the religious leaders, calling them blind guides and hypocrites. He says, "Behold, your house is being left to you desolate!"[4] That is intense! This is not going to be a good day it seems. First the fig tree didn't satisfy His hunger and meet Him at the level that it promised, and now He seems to be divorcing Himself and His Father from everything going on in the temple. Today isn't a day to be on His bad side. You are unsure how to process all this.

Condemning the Religious Leaders

He has really stirred up a hornet's nest in the outer precincts of the temple, outraged the scribes and Pharisees and seems to be unconcerned for His own welfare. Things are at a boiling point. You are certain that any minute the temple guards will come and take Him away. But not one reaches out a hand to touch Him, even though He has pronounced woes on them.

The tone of His voice when He pronounced those woes was just like the tone of His voice when He cursed the fig tree. He can be tough, but you have never quite seen Him that tough. Nevertheless, He is never malicious. He is grieved, and it seems as if His heart is always being broken.

You stand nearby and watch as He weeps over the city. He feels deeply about the state of things, but when you see Him weep with deep sobs, it is gut-wrenching for you. He weeps for a city that does not recognize who He is, and you feel the power of His travail in the deepest places of your own soul.

This is the second time you can't handle the way He is weeping. He also wept at the tomb of Lazarus. Somehow you knew that it wasn't Lazarus He was weeping about. You hear that same groan come out of Him when He weeps for the city. It is unsettling, and it stirs up things inside you for which you are not prepared.

After dusk, you hit the rocky trail back to Bethany. He prefers staying outside the intense environment of the city proper whenever evening comes. He needs a place to retreat and regroup. Martha and Mary's house provides the perfect hideaway. It is dark when you arrive at the edge of Bethany to retire for the night.

Early the next morning, as is His custom, He gets up before the crack of dawn. He has already been out alone to pray when He comes to awaken you and the rest. You aren't sure what awaits you today in the big city, but you are feeling knots in your stomach already. Circumstances are intensifying, and any minute the whole thing can come falling down on you.

Believe and Not Doubt

As you leave Bethany to return to the city, you notice the same lone fig tree that the Master had spoken to the previous morning. Yesterday, its beautiful foliage grabbed your attention. Today it is dried up, withered from the roots for lack of moisture.

Now, you have seen plants wither and die over the course of time, but this one had been healthy, vibrant and green yesterday morning—and it is withered and dead today. It is beyond your comprehension.

You get His attention and say, "Master, look! The fig tree You cursed has withered from the roots up!"

Even though you think you are making a statement, your heart is raising a question. The intent of your communication is the outcome you receive. You aren't saying, "Look at what happened!" You are really asking, "How did that happen? How did You do that?"

He hears your intent and responds beyond your superficial communication. His response is simple, straightforward and commanding: "Have faith in God!"

That's it? Have faith in God? you ask yourself. He then explains that it does not matter who does the talking. If anyone has faith in God and tells a mountain to be removed and cast into the sea, it will be removed. The only requirement to perform such a miracle is that you need to believe and not doubt in your hearts.[5]

In your heart you say, "Fig trees maybe, even though it is still hard to believe, but mountains? Never!"

He compares a small fig tree to a large mountain. But for Him, size of the obstacle is not the issue. Instead it's the essential quality and congruence of speech.

Congruence of Speech

Congruence is an essential element in communication. If I answer yes to a question while shaking my head no at the same time, then my communication is not congruent.

If I invite you to speak, but at the same time I put my index finger over my lips as though to say, "Shhhh," then my communication is not congruent. If I say, "This sounds fishy," then my words are not congruent. How can something *sound* fishy? Something can only smell fishy.

Yet how many times have you heard someone say exactly that? When what you are feeling and what you are saying are not the same, and when what you are thinking is not aligned with what you are doing, you are in a place of incongruence. Often when incongruence is present, doubt is hiding somewhere in the shadows and needs to be faced, addressed and dealt with.

I believe this issue of incongruence has been overlooked in the incident of the fig tree. When Jesus cursed the fig tree, He was addressing the mixed messages we communicate. That is the reason that mountains and roadblocks cause us to stay stuck in places that deny our real potential.

The fig tree was not congruent. It was "saying" one thing by its leaves and doing something else by its lack of fruit. What it said and what it did were not consistent. The result: It offered an illusion of hope, but the outcome of that hope was disappointment and dissatisfaction.

As Simon, discussing this matter of congruence with Jesus might have sounded like the following discussion.

Faith and Congruence

"If you have faith like a grain of a mustard seed, than you have all that is necessary to move a mountain," the Master said.

You can't seem to comprehend that, so you question Him. How can a tiny little mustard seed move a mountain?

"Ah, Simon, I hear you! You are looking at the size of the mustard seed and comparing it to the size of the mountain. But I am looking at the substance of the mustard seed and the substance of the mountain."

"What do you mean, Master?"

"Simon, the mustard seed is a living thing, although it is dormant until placed in the ground. Under the tiny shell of that seed is an encoded destiny, an innate wisdom and a blueprint. These are all the necessary ingredients for it to become the tallest tree in the garden.

"That tiny little seed is only the shell of the substance of the blueprint. It will become what it knows it was meant to be.

"Have you noticed that rocks cannot stop the growth of a tree once its seed is planted? The life of that seed triumphs over the dead material of the rock. Life always triumphs over inactivity! When your words come from a place of deep intention and congruent communication, they will also contain the power of life. That's why it is so important that you say what you mean and mean what you say.

"When you do, you will discover a power beyond yourself

working through your words that will bring about the desires of your heart. Don't you remember that I told you that My words are spirit and life?"

"Yes, I do, Sir. But how do I get to a place where I say what I mean and mean what I say? And what does that have to do with moving the mountain that Jerusalem is built on? Master, do You really think anyone can move a mountain?"

"Simon, an hour is coming when this mountain will no longer be called the mountain of the Lord. My Father is building a new mountain, and this one will be removed. Don't you remember My telling you about your new name and your new nature? That new name and nature is in union with My Father. You are a living stone, and I am the cornerstone.

"Daniel saw a small stone that was carved out of an existing mountain without the aid of a man's hand. That stone was a living seed. That seed represented the promised seed of Abraham. That seed, which is a stone, will grow to become a new mountain that will fill the entire earth.

"Simon, there is only one thing remaining in order for that seed, that living stone, to pass through in order for that mountain over there where Passover is being celebrated right now to be removed. The seed has to fall into the ground and die. Its outer shell has to be cracked open so that the life inside it and the blueprint it carries can begin to break up the old mountain. Then it can begin to replace it with living stones that it will reproduce by its death and burial.

"Except a grain of wheat fall into the ground and die, Simon, it remains alone. However, if it dies it bears much fruit.[6] Its outcomes multiply because it is being congruent. What is intended that is carried in the seed is congruent with its willingness to lose its outer shell and let the real life inside be manifest. The shell is only there for protection until that life is ready to be released. If you hang on to the shell, you never become congruent with your intention.

"Simon, son of John, you are Peter, yet there needs to come one final passage for you to become congruent. Don't be afraid, though. I'll walk through that path with you in the same way that I have walked with you on the beach, on the water, through the corrections, the rebukes and the affirmations. I will bring you safely to the other side. You have to trust Me beyond the shadow of doubt!"

What is to give light

must first

endure

What is to give light must first endure burning.

—VIKTOR FRANKL

Chapter 13

Finding Inner Congruence

It is not always easy to know or admit to ourselves what it is we really want. But congruence does not come without genuine honesty and transparency.

Like Simon, we do not say, "Wow! Look at what happened to that fig tree!" Instead we are asking, "How did You do that?" More importantly, we are also asking, "Can I do that as well?" Perhaps at the same time something inside us is telling us, "I can't do that, so why even bother trying?"

The "how to" requires that we come to grips with those parts of ourselves that are sometimes hard to get a handle on because they are hiding in the shadows. We need to go into the place of the shadows, even if it feels uncomfortable.

As a child, I can remember being afraid of the dark. I can remember as an adult being in situations where there was little natural light at night and where I didn't know what was lurking in the shadows, and I became filled with fear. Darkness threatens our existence even though it is part of our life experience.

From the beginning, everything began in the "deep and dark." Light came to separate it out, but even after separating it out, the light did not eliminate the darkness. It simply put limits and boundaries on it. From that moment on, darkness could go so far and no farther.

Facing the Darkness

Somewhere within us we need to learn how to trust God that the darkness is set within limits. For us to become what we were meant to become it is vital to face the darkness head-on and not avoid it.

It isn't all that easy to do. Haven't we all dug in our heels and had to be dragged like screaming children to the dentist's office. It was not the first visit that scared us—we did not know what to expect. But after we experienced the dentist's drill, we become resistant to the next visit. Once the dentist puts that drill in our mouth, life with the dentist is something to be avoided even if he or she does have our best interest at heart.

Not everything in the dark is to be feared. There are treasures that are hidden in the darkness.[1] I can remember sneaking up into the attic in our home on Bement Avenue. It was off limits as far as Dad was concerned, but curiosity and Dad's edict made it all the more appealing. I was willing to face my fear of the dark—and for sure, it was dark up there—to find out what was under all those old bed sheets. When I got up there and found old toys, pictures and knick knacks, I felt like a pirate of the Caribbean who had just found buried treasure on the shores of a deserted island.

Darkness and light are alike to God, but not to us. We have a natural aversion to the dark, and for good reason. Much is associated with the dark that is painful, demonic, destructive and oppressive. Who would volunteer to go into the dark without being coerced? Yet the only way to eliminate the dark is to shed light on it. As long as things stay in the dark, we give them power.

Hiding our unfinished business is what gives it power. Secret addictions have power because they remain secret. Secret fears have power because we hide them in the dark. We shove things below the level of our conscious awareness and cover the trap door to the basement with a rug so that no one ever looks down there.

A dear friend came to a conference a few years back. He was struggling with an inner picture he saw of his "internal house" in a vision while he was praying. In the vision he kept having to go "down to the basement," and he did not want to go because it was messy down there.

I tried to help him interpret what the symbolism meant, and we made some progress. However, he was not quite able to clean up the mess in the basement, which was his unfinished business. Every once in a while he still reminds me of it. We both smile and reflect on how often unfinished business can cause us to get stuck in the basement where little light comes in and shadows rule the environment.

Dottie Rambo wrote the song "In the Valley He Restoreth My Soul." Let's get back into the parable to experience the healing and release awaiting us once we have faced our own darkness.

Preparing for Passover

The Master sends you and John early that Thursday morning to prepare for the Passover Seder. His instructions are simple and strange: "When you enter the village, you will meet a man carrying a water jar."

That is enough to disturb you to begin with, for as far as you are concerned, real men don't carry water jars. That is a woman's job, and everyone in your town knows it—everyone in your culture knows it. What man in his right mind would do what is women's work?

The day is starting off just great; already you are being stretched to go where you have never gone. It will not be hard to spot a man carrying a water jar because everyone else carrying them that morning will have soft eyes, soft hair and soft skin. Just look for the one with the beard and the rough exterior, and you've got your man!

It strikes you as strange, though, because ever since you started hanging out with the Master all sorts of strange coincidences seem to happen in your life. It is as if these meaningful "chance encounters" have secret meanings that are always appropriate to where you are at that moment of time in your walk with Him. He calls them "happy accidents on purpose."

"Whatever," you used to respond back. You can't get over it, though. Why would a man carry a water jar? Worse yet, once you find him, you have to be *seen* following him, which means that you will be identified with him. Don't you just love being challenged to go where your lower nature refuses to go? What are people going to think if they see you, a man's man, Simon, son of John, walking with a man who would stoop so low as to perform the task of a woman? What will the neighbors think?

However, if you are going to prepare the Passover, he is the one who will lead you to the wealthy owner of a house with a large and thoroughly furnished room on the second floor that will be big enough to hold twelve men and a rabbi. Sure enough, you see the bearded guy amidst all the women in the town square. He looks awfully silly with that water jar on his head. It is a bit humorous to see, but he doesn't seem to mind, even though the women are also looking at him as if he is strange.

You and John walk up and want to introduce yourselves, but before you can get the words out, he says, "Follow me." Those words have a familiar ring to them. They are compelling, and his demeanor for a servant is quite disarming. You still keep looking over your shoulder and in every direction as you follow him, staring back at those who stare at you. You aren't going to let them stare at you without giving it right back; after all, you have a reputation to maintain. Nobody is going to mess with you!

The man with the water jar leads you straight to the house of the wealthy householder and up the outside stairwell to a door leading into a very large and thoroughly furnished upper room. There is nothing to go out and get except the lamb and the wine. The candles are there, as well as the table and all the utensils. The man who led you there places the water jar carefully at the threshold of the doorway to the large upper room and then bids you farewell.

Once your task is completed, you leave with John. On your way out the door you move the water jar slightly so that no one will trip over it. You stick it way in the corner so that the passageway to the door is totally unobstructed.

Celebrating Passover

That night at dusk everyone shuffles up the stairs and sits down. While you and John were away, John's mom approached Jesus on behalf of her sons, asking for the highest and most prestigious positions for them. She wanted them to sit on His right hand and His left, for after all, they were the best qualified for the job.

You didn't talk to John much after that because you are sure that he and James put their mom up to it. Of the inner circle, you are the best qualified to be the closest to Jesus in the new order of things.

None of you pay any attention to the water jar that is there, especially since you stuck it in the corner out of sight. You all came in and sat down, ready to eat. But Jesus, who has an eye for detail, saw where you placed the water jar.

Jesus gets up from the table before praying, takes off His robe and puts a large towel around His waist. He goes over to the water jar and brings it out in the open in full view. He then dips His hands in the water, kneels down and, grabbing your feet, begins to wash them.

"Gosh, Lord, what are You doing this for? This isn't important. Besides, this kind of work is for slaves to do, not You. You have a reputation to preserve! Don't You care what the rest of these guys think about You?"

"If I don't wash your feet, you can't travel any further with Me. This will be the end of the road."

"No, Lord, I don't want to stop traveling with You. Go ahead, and don't just do my feet, wash my hands and my head as well!"

Aren't you being obsessive? One minute you are embarrassed because you can't stand to see Him doing a menial task. You are concerned about His reputation and how others perceive Him. Or are you really concerned about your own reputation? Perhaps you are projecting onto Him your own need to be seen in the proper light. Maybe you aren't concerned about the others at all.

The next minute you are so concerned about not being able to travel with Him any longer that you don't care what anyone else thinks. Let Him give you a bath. You are so driven by your needs and out of touch with where you are that it is almost a comedy of errors to watch you go through the changes you go through.

Why was a man carrying a water jar anyway? What was in that serendipitous event that was being hinted at? When the man said, "Follow me," and sounded a lot like the Man whom you have been following, why did you not understand the meaning behind where he led you and what he left for you at the doorway? Why didn't you secure someone to take care of the ceremonial washing of the hands and feet before the Seder?

How many details do you miss when God invites you to an experience? When you are not prepared to face and to deal with your inner drives and unmet needs, you cannot see clearly. Why are there moments in your life when you project onto others—and perhaps even onto God—what you refuse to face in yourself?

Are you aware of how many times you have judged the values of others because they aren't your own? It seems to you that the man with the water jar valued fulfilling his purpose more than he valued how other people perceived him. He did what he did because of the Master of the house.

The Servant Spirit

Isn't it interesting that the Holy Spirit never brings attention to Himself? Instead, He focuses attention on Jesus. Although He is God, He takes the position of a servant to carry the water of life. He leads you to the Father's house where He invites you to enter into a large and thoroughly furnished upper room, a higher place, and then He leaves you to decide how you will prepare for the supper of the Lamb.

When He leads you, are you aware of how much unfinished business you are still dealing with, how much you are driven by your needs to be seen, appreciated, recognized and honored? It is not pleasant to face such difficult truths about yourself, sure, but do you really and truly want to be healed and travel where the Master is traveling?

Washing Simon's Feet

When Jesus washed Simon's feet, He said, "If I do not wash you,

you have no part with Me."[2] The word picture in the Greek language is that of a fellow traveler down the road. If you want to get to the place of transformation, the place of metamorphosis is a process you have yet to experience. You have to allow Him to wash your feet and get you ready for the walk you are about to take through the valley of shadows. Your future depends on it. Are you ready to go further and be healed? Only go there if you are ready to be healed.

Imagery of the Passover Meal

After everyone, including Judas, has his feet washed, you all proceed with the meal. He changes the rules again and does what you have never seen done in your family celebration of the Passover Seder. An empty seat was traditionally placed for Elijah as well as the cup of Elijah at the table. He gives thanks for the meal and blesses it. He opens the napkin you had carefully and meticulously folded earlier in the day, creating three pockets in it where you placed three loaves of bread. One was placed in each pocket, just as your father and mother did all the years you grew up in their house. He lays it flat on the table.

The threefold napkin is now open with all three loaves sticking out of the pockets, folded over, and visible to all of you. He reaches down and takes the middle loaf. That is new. Your dad never reached for the middle loaf, and even though you were little when Grandpa died, you still can remember the Passover holidays when he officiated, and you don't ever remember him reaching for the middle loaf. They either grabbed the first loaf or the last one, never the one in the middle. What is He doing now?

Why were there three loaves anyway? The rabbis always told us that they represented Abraham, Isaac and Jacob. Tonight, though, things are being made clear. You hear Him say to John before He stands up to bless the bread, "I am about to bring things out of the shadows and reveal the substance of things to come!"

When He lifts up the middle loaf He says, "This loaf, the middle loaf, is My body..." While He is speaking, He breaks it in half and continues without missing a beat by saying, "...which is broken for you."

You feel something tear inside you as His hands break the bread. It occurs to you that what He is saying and what He is doing are *congruent!* The message grabs you right in the heart. As He breaks the bread, you feel unseen hands grabbing hold of your innermost being to pry it open, but you resist. You don't allow it to happen. It is not the time and place to open up your heart. You have enough pressure on you already, and you certainly don't need any more.

One of You Will Betray Me

Then He says, "You aren't all with Me. One of you is being driven by demonic power and will betray Me!"

John leans over and asks Him a question. You are curious to know what Jesus told him. You wonder if He told him who was going to betray Him. You don't want to know because when He said that Satan was at work in one of you, you instantly recalled your conversation three and a half months ago on that large rock. You wonder if He is talking about you. Your mind rocks and reels as you process your unwanted feelings and fears. You are oblivious to the fact that Judas, after having been given a piece of bread dipped in wine by the Master, mysteriously leaves the table and never comes back. You are so preoccupied with yourself that you aren't present to the moment. Yet somewhere in the back of your mind where you are sorting through your memories and your feelings, you seem to recall hearing Jesus say to Judas, "What you do, do quickly!" But you have no idea what that was all about.

If that isn't enough, He quotes a verse from one of the prophets.

It seems to be from an obscure passage in Zechariah that the rabbis couldn't quite interpret. It is something like, "Slay the shepherd and scatter the sheep!"[3]

He implies that it means that on that very night, He is going to be struck down and you are all going to scatter and forsake Him. By this time you are feeling so scattered on the inside after the day's events that the comment about Satan pushes you over the edge. Your motto is "Save yourself no matter what!" You are going to preserve your seemingly spotless image for yourself in His eyes regardless. The events of the last few weeks and months and then years flash before you in a split second.

The next thing you know you jump to your feet. In a spirit of defiance you look around at everyone else, for you want them all to know who you are. Then you look at Jesus and point your index finger, declaring, "Though all these leave You (and you point your finger at every one of them as you circle the table), I will never leave You."

The Caterpillar Must Die

In essence you are reminding Him of who He said you were. You are Peter, a large living stone, and He is going to give you the keys to the kingdom. Whatever you lock up in heaven will be locked up, and whatever you lock up on earth will be locked up. He said you would kick in the gates of hell—you and Him of course.

You aren't ready for what comes next. It hits you broadside like a cannonball hitting the hull of a battleship.

"Simon, Simon."

He hasn't called you Simon in months. Why now? He doesn't stop there, though. He goes on to say, "Satan has requested permission from My Father to sift you the same way that wheat is sifted to separate the wheat from the chaff. He wants to sift you to the core to prove there isn't much in you, that you are all surface and there is no substance to your character. He claims that you are a tare and not wheat. He claims that once the outer shell of the wheat kernel is removed—which is the façade that you so readily project to preserve your reputation—there won't be anything left of you at all. And Simon, My Father has granted Satan permission to do what he is demanding!"

You muster up every last bit of emotional strength within you to stand on your feet and not show any sense of being shaken. You are not about to seem weak in the eyes of your peers at this challenge of Satan. You swallow every bit of the emotional distress that is coming up from somewhere deep inside and try to take it in. You feel rejected, but you can't admit it to yourself. You feel naked and exposed, but you still have your clothing on. You have been stripped in the presence of your peers, and it is too much to bear. Your heart sinks into a place of despair while your countenance stays stiff and rigid.

The Master allows you to process what you just "heard." He knows that what is happening on the outside of you is not congruent with what is taking place on the inside.

He then says, "Simon"—there He goes again calling you by your former name—"you will deny you ever knew Me!"

That's enough! He can't say that. You have been faithful to Him through thick and thin. You heard Him say so just a little while ago during the supper. He wanted to share this Passover with you and the rest because you stood by Him in all His tests. He knows better than to say that you will deny you ever knew Him.

"I'll never deny you!"

The words come out, but there is a break in your voice. Your emotional pain is showing; you can't mask it. It sounds as if He is saying that you are going to fail the test. The worst thing you can ever imagine is to fail at something. You have to prove you are flawless.

As He watches the words fall from your lips and feels the pain in your voice, He continues, for love does not spare us from facing ourselves and dealing with what is hiding in the shadows. The only way to freedom is through the valley of shadows.

"Simon, before the rooster crows once in the morning you will have denied knowing Me three times!"

In other words, when you hear the wake-up call, it will reawaken your conscience to this present moment and invite you to face yourself with all your darkness.

You are undone, angry and fearful, and you are definitely withdrawing yourself from the activities at the table. Everyone is as quiet as a church mouse and is looking at you. You resume an eating position at the table because you no longer want to be the center of attention, and you don't want anyone to look at you anymore. You wish you could crawl into a hole and die (since you go to extremes quite readily and easily). He then says one more thing. As His mouth opens, your eyes meet His gaze, and He looks as He did when you first saw Him on the beach. You fear what is coming next, but His eyes suggest that it will be tender. When He opens His mouth, His speech is soothing once again. He is as congruent now as He was a moment ago when He was correcting you.

"But I have prayed for you, Simon. I have sought the Father on your behalf. As hard as it may be to get to this awareness at the moment, don't let your heart be troubled. Believe in God, and also believe in Me. In My Father's house there are many rooms that are as big as this one we are in right now, or even bigger. There are appointments and positions that are awaiting you there. I am going to prepare a place for you and the rest that where I am you may be also.[4]

"After you have been converted and become congruent, and after you have left all the behaviors and beliefs of your former identity, you will be able to give strength to your brothers. You want to be a leader amongst your peers. I promised I would make you that, but the caterpillar has to die for the butterfly to rise!"

Drinking the Cup of the Master

After the lamb is eaten, He reaches for Elijah's cup. He breaks the rules again. He says, "This cup (the one you thought was Elijah's cup) is the New Covenant in My blood. Drink from it, every one of you." He leaves the fourth cup for some reason, and you sing a hymn from the psalms of David. You are still processing everything that He said, but you remember singing the words, "Bind Me with cords unto the altar of sacrifice."

The only way we can pass through the valley of shadows safely is to partake of the cup of the Master. That cup is the stuff dreams are made of, and it is also the stuff of life. For Joseph it was the key to a reunion with his father. Many, many years later another Joseph, one from Arimathea, was said to have taken it on a journey. There legend says that it was well hidden and became the supreme quest. The search for the Holy Grail became the legend of Arthur and the Knights of the Round Table.

The drinking of the cup is an acknowledgment of the death that covers us as we face the shadows of our own death. Christ's sacrifice on our behalf makes it possible for us to face our own rite of passage without fear. Because of the blood of the New Covenant, the death angel that awaits us in the Kidron Valley (or dark valley in Hebrew) will pass over us. Because of the blood of Christ, the angel of death cannot touch us. That death will touch Him instead, for this is what the fourth cup was all about.

As you follow Him together with the others, you cross the Kidron Valley. It is His favorite place to go and pray. A garden there, called Gethsemane, meaning the oil press, is a place where He often finds comfort and solace. Ripe olives are pressed here to get the precious oil that is used for food, light, healing, cosmetics and, most importantly, for the anointing of prophets, priests and kings.

You and the other disciples know this place well, for you have been here with Him many times before. Here He will drink the fourth cup alone, the cup that will break over Him as He swallows it with all its fury.

After slaying the lamb that was sacrificed for the people's sins, the high priest would lay his hands on the head of a goat, called the scapegoat. This symbolized the mystical transference of the nation's sins. He would then order the priests to drive the scapegoat out into the wilderness over the edge of a high ravine where it would fall into a dark abyss. This symbolized banishment forever from the presence of God, never to be seen again.

There in Gethsemane the Master prays three times for the fourth cup to pass from Him. The notion of not only being the sacrificed lamb, but of also becoming the scapegoat and being sent to hell for the sins of the nation where He would be separated from the unconditional love of His Father, is all too much to bear.

Dying for someone else's sins is one thing. Becoming their sin, suffering torment and separation so that they might be in union with the Father and never be separated was a deep issue. Would He be willing to be separated from the Father and to undergo torment so that those for whom He suffered might never be separated from His Father?

He loves the Father more than life itself, and He could not imagine ever being separated from this One He lived for. Asking Him to become everything His Father and He detested, with the possibility of suffering eternally with no end in sight so that others could live forever in His Father's delight, is an unspeakable test. Can that be what He is being asked to do? Is the cup that devastating?

The Hour of Temptation

That hour is now fully upon Him. He wept at the tomb of Lazarus, and He wept over the city a few days previous. Now His third season of weeping is upon Him, for He Himself will now enter into the valley of the shadow of death. He will walk that valley uncovered, unprotected and given into the hands of the powers of hell itself with no support whatsoever from His Father. He will be forsaken and abandoned so that all those who drank the cup could be spared.

They will live with the assurance of never being forsaken. He will enter into the experience of being forsaken on their behalf. He will experience the depths of that separation in the valley of shadows. He will find every demonic image, every distorted and broken image and every corrupted and perverted image. By His permission, the uncleanness that never touched Him will attempt to drive Him to the very limits of sanity. Yet, as He enters that dark valley of shadows, He Himself will discover the rod and staff of comfort even while the outer shell of His humanity undergoes death.

He will overthrow every principality and power that have dug their foul claws into His soul and find that they have nothing to hold onto. He will cast off every last vestige of their claims to Him and His humanity, and He will cry out in triumph and breathe His last human breath.

As He distances Himself from the rest, He invites you, James and John to come closer and enter into a place of exchange with God. You are exhausted and about to fall off to sleep when you hear Him cry out in a loud voice, "Let this cup pass from Me."

You could have sworn He said it at least three times, but you are so weary you drift off to sleep wondering what cup He is referring to.

Betrayal

When you awaken, you are startled out of sleep by the sound of approaching feet marching in cadence. A legion of temple guards with priests and scribes is walking briskly up the mountainside. You cannot make them out through the shadows. But as they approach, you recognize who it is: Judas is leading the charge.

Anger rises within you, and you unsheathe the sword at your side, gripping the cold steel handle with your thumb and the palm of your hand and wrapping its leather strap around your wrist with the other hand. As Judas comes close, he kisses the Master with the kiss of betrayal and steps out of the way. Something in you wants to drive the sword through him, but you find yourself restrained from doing so; you actually are bewildered by his actions.

Malchus, a young slave of Caiaphas, gets too close to the Master. Instantly, without a moment's notice, your swift hand removes the sword from its sheath, and in one stroke you cut off his right ear. Jesus tells you to put your sword away, and He reaches down and picks up the flesh that you cut off from the young man's head. He touches him at the point where it was severed and heals him instantly. Malchus, overwhelmed by the sword and the loss of his ear, is now deeply moved by the touch of the Master.

In a calm voice the Master asks whom the temple guards are seeking. They reply, "Jesus of Nazareth."

At that point, He says, "I am."

The entire cohort, including the priests and scribes, fall over backward in the presence of the Lord of glory. You remember what that felt like. At significant moments you too lost your balance when something came out of Him as He spoke. Twice He asks the question, and twice they fall over. After the second time, He simply puts out both of His hands and allows Himself to be bound and tied and led away to be questioned.

Denial and Betrayal

They lead Him to the house of Caiaphas, where He is brought into the inner court of the house to be interrogated. You follow at a distance and stand outside in the outer courtyard. The night is getting cold, so you begin to warm your hands at a nearby fire that was started by a slave girl.

The fear and anger from the past number of hours has caused your love to wax cold and your passion to wane. When your love waxes cold, your internal fire begins to die; you need an external fire to keep your hands doing what they were meant to do.

The slave girl can't keep her eyes off of you. Others are all around the fire, but she chooses to stare with a penetrating gaze.

As she looks at you, she says, "You are with Him, aren't you?"

"No, I am not," you reply.

Then a man opposite the blaze stares back at you. "I've seen you with Him in the streets before!"

"Man, you have never seen me with Him," you snap back, sternly rebuking him.

Things quiet down a bit as the questioning continues in the inner court of the high priest's house. False witnesses are there accusing Him of things He had not done, twisting His words. They make it sound as if He said things that He never said.

Another man keeps looking at the Man on trial, and then he turns to you by the fire. Without hesitation he says, "There is no doubt about it; you are one of His disciples!"

Your anger gets the best of you, and you curse the man. Once again you deny ever having had a relationship with the Master. Immediately, the rooster echoes the voice of your violated conscience. Then, without missing a beat, the Master turns around. He has felt your presence behind Him the entire time and has been present to you through this part of the valley even though He seemed distant.

Those penetrating yet loving eyes meet you from across the courtyard, and you are undone. There is no condemnation in His look, only grief and unconditional love.

He knows you better than you know yourself. He knows those tendencies in you that you refuse to admit are there, and He still cares. He knows your ability to justify yourself and is not shocked. Yet, even in the hour of His own death, you are so valuable to Him that He sees you and hears your cry.

It hits you like a ton of bricks. You have failed the One who gave everything for you to live a life of meaning and abundance. You can't face Him, and you can't face those around the fire. You can't face yourself. You aren't the person you projected yourself as being. You realize that for all your effort you were living a less than genuine existence. Your intentions may have been good, but your actions were not congruent with what was really going on in your heart. You had refused to accept the parts of you that were in the shadows because bringing them to the light was not a pleasant experience.

Running Away From Yourself

All you can do is run. You get up from the fire and you run. You run hard, and you run fast. You run out of the city, out past the dusty trail toward Bethany. You are running, running, running. Where are you going?

As you are trying to retrace your steps, your memory races back over every significant moment when you refused to deal with the issues that He brought to light. You retrace your steps while your heart seems to have unleashed a flood of buried emotions.

Waves of fear and anger give way to deep sobs that rise out of a broken and wounded spirit. You don't even know where all the pain is coming from, but it just keeps coming. When you think you have cried all there is to cry, somewhere from some deep place below the layers you have just exposed comes another outburst. You weep so bitterly that the bitterness in your soul can be tasted on your lips.

You begin to heave and retch as you release all that poison from inside your system. The hours pass, and you find yourself lying on the side of the road under the withered branches of a cursed fig tree. As the morning breaks, you are exhausted and weak. You wonder how you arrived at that place. Somehow you know that it is an appropriate place for you to be. That fig tree is mirroring for you what your life has been up until this point. You had the appearance of being able to feed and nurture, heal and cure the hunger of those who passed by you on the road of life. But when people got close and looked beyond your external appearance, they realized there was nothing but leaves.

Becoming Genuine

A voice is speaking to you now, letting you know how false and phony you have been and driving the point home that you have failed. Funny, you never paid too much attention before to the tone of that voice as you laughed it off. Now it dawns on you that the voice has been driving you to perform all your life. But it is nothing like the voice of the One who said He loved you no matter what.

You also realize that every time you judged the values of your brothers and sisters you allowed that voice to speak through you. Even though you can't seem to shake this voice, you feel separated on the inside from it for the first time in your life. It's there, but it isn't you. It used to be you, but when you heaved up all that pain and let go of all that bitterness, your own voice became calmer and clearer. The accusing voice became disassociated from your own.

The Road of Sorrow

It is about the third or fourth hour of the day, judging by where the sun is in the sky. You pick yourself up and begin to head back toward the city. You enter the center of the city to find the crowds are yelling to Pilate to release a criminal and murderer, madly screaming to crucify the Man you call Master.

From the back of the crowd you lift your voice, "Take me instead." But you are so weakened that no one can hear you. You watch as they lead Him away to be crucified.

His head, bloodied from the three-inch thorns woven into a crown and driven deep into His skull, is swelled to twice its normal size. They are stripping off His robe, the seamless one that His mother had made for Him, the one thing that was His connection to His natural life and His home in Nazareth. As they strip Him, you notice that His back is plowed with deep furrows, apparently from a scourging. You wish you could have been there to stop them as pain goes even deeper into your already wounded heart.

Those furrows expose the very tender parts of His internal workings. His flesh has been ripped open. Every layer of the outer skin is ripped to shreds where the cat-o'-nine tails did its demonic work. When they lay that large wooden beam across His torn back, you feel His agony as the splinters go deep into those open wounds and brush against the exposed flesh. You wince in pain and try to get through the crowd. It's no use; the guards aren't letting anyone get close, and you haven't got an ounce of strength to fight your way anywhere.

As they go up the road of sorrows and pain, your heart is now suffering, but not for yourself. It is suffering as if you were the one in His shoes. You feel the weight of that heavy cross and the pain of those thorns in your brow. Your head aches, and your eyes go in and out of focus. You are at the point of being delirious and wanting to pass out because of the pain. At one point you drop to the ground from the weight of it all. As if out of nowhere, like an angel sent from heaven, a dark-skinned man from Africa breaks through the crowd and offers to carry the cross for Him. You feel the weight of that heavy burden become lighter. You aren't in this alone, even though your suffering is unique to your individual journey.

You realize you can't carry His cross; you have to carry your own. Somehow, that black man realized that he was carrying his own cross, although he was carrying the one belonging to a Man he had never known before.

Facing the Agony

You hear the weeping and the travail of the multitudes. The little child whom He had raised from the dead is there with her father, Jairus. The widow of Nain is there with her only son, whom He had given back to her. The lepers whom He had healed—they are in the crowd. You hear their pleas for mercy, but Caiaphas is smiling glee-fully, and the scribes and Pharisees are gloating under their breath, walking in pomp and arrogance, feeling self-justified through it all.

You remember you have brothers, but where are they? What are they feeling? Where is John?

"Have you seen James or John, the sons of Zebedee?" you ask one of the crowd who knows who they are.

"No, I haven't seen them," is the reply.

The procession approaches the garbage dump outside the city, past the Refuse Gate. You can smell the stench of human waste and the rotting leftovers of many days of celebration. As they lead Him up the side of a hill called "the place of the skull," you watch them remove His outer garments, His seamless robe and His sandals.

Four guards each take an arm or a foot. A large spike is driven through each wrist. You can hear Him agonize with greater pain as you feel the nerve endings in your own wrists coil back in horrific agony. Then you watch as the two men at His feet hold one foot atop the other and drove a spike straight through the two, the spike crushing His heels as it rivets Him to that large and heavy wooden Roman tau. If ever a tree was cursed, this one is it, and the fruit on the tree is now cursed.

They hoist Him up and drop that wooden cross into the earth—you can feel every bone in His body jerk and jolt. He struggles to breathe. You can feel the strain as He strains to catch His breath. He rests the weight of His broken and bleeding body on the spikes through His wrists and feet to lift Himself up enough to catch a breath. With every breath He takes He utters something worth remembering.

Your heart is breaking open. Those invisible hands that you resisted when He broke bread the night before are now breaking open your heart again. The tears are coming out of you from such a deep place that you cannot control the sobbing.

You feel totally helpless, totally worthless and totally powerless. For the first time in your life those feelings you have buried so deeply that you wouldn't have to face them are there out in the open, exposed for all to see. At least that's how you feel, and there is not a thing you can do about it. Everything that was hiding in the shadows is now being brought into the light.

You are enraged at the soldiers. No sooner do they drop that cross into its standing position in the earth then they start gambling for His garments right there in front of Him. They are His only possessions—His outer garments and sandals and a beautiful seamless robe that His mother had made Him.

Your anger is boiling. You forget about your own weakness for a moment and want to cry out about the injustice, when all of a sudden from the top of that cross, the Man you call Master, anticipating the need for some healing in others and in you, cried out.

"Father, forgive them, for they don't know what they are doing."

All the anger in you dissolves as you marvel at how this Man is totally congruent in all that He says and does. He passes no judgment. He only offers a cry for forgiveness. How can He do that?

Thieves by His Side

While both thieves on either side have been mocking Him, one stops. He had been to some of His campaigns and heard Him speak of a heavenly kingdom, but he was not a pushover for another scam from another false prophet.

But now the thief realizes he has become everything he wished he hadn't. He learned how to steal in order to survive. He learned how to hate in order to live. He learned how to cheat to get by. He learned to silence the inner voice of tenderness because no one really cared. His heart was so hard that he had no time for God.

But somehow in that moment, when Jesus cries out and requests that forgiveness be released, his heart is broken. Just like you, he sees beyond the now broken flesh of that Man. By an act of grace, he realizes that this is indeed the Messiah. He stops hurling his abuse and turns to the other criminal.

He says, "You and I deserve what we are getting, but this Man hasn't done anything worthy of death."

How does he know that? That could not have come by flesh and blood—you know that yourself. Someone is talking to him, even as he is passing through the valley of shadows. He sees Christ for who He is, and He asks only one thing: "When You come into Your kingdom, please remember the me I was intended to be, not the me I have become. I don't need anything except to know that I am not forgotten. I have messed up my opportunities, but I know by now seeing You that there is more to life than what I have lived. I know You are a king, and kings have the power to execute decrees. I deserve death, but don't forget who I could have been when You inherit what is rightfully yours. Please keep me in remembrance!"

Your Master, true to His nature and promise, turns to him and says, "Today you will be with Me in paradise. I promise!"

It is all too much to take in. Suddenly it gets really dark, black as coal, like the dark night of the soul you have been passing through. The air grows very, very still. And with the darkness comes a silence.

Your memory races back to the story of the night when darkness fell on all the land of Egypt and the death angel passed over. This is the valley of the shadow of death. It seems as if it lasts for eternity. When the darkness falls, His eyes suddenly change. For the first time you see terror and fear. Your Master is fearful and terrified. You panic inside because you have never seen Him out of control. His eye movements are rapid. They go up, they go to the right, they go to the left, they go down—and no matter where they go there is no diminishing of the terror and fear. Then all of a sudden, in a loud shrill voice He cries out, "My God, My God, WHY?"

It is as if He has entered into the pain of every why that was uttered by every human being born of Adam's race. "Why the pain?" "Why the suffering?" "Why the torment?" "Why the agony?" "Why the loss?" "Why death?" "Why misery?" "Why the sense of separation from God?" "Why the feelings of abandonment and isolation?" "Why have You forsaken Me?" "I don't deserve this!" "Why do I have to endure this?" "This is tormenting, and it doesn't make any sense!" "If You are a God of love, why allow Me to see what I am seeing and endure what I am enduring?" "Why is this happening to Me?"

There is no answer, only silence. Just as in your life when you pass through the valley of shadows, there is no answer. There is only a profound sense of abandonment and darkness in that valley.

Why? is the most unaffirming question that can be raised through human lips. Have you also discovered that when people are suffering and they ask why, you feel powerless to give them an answer? There is no answer for the why. You simply have to experience it for yourself. There is never an answer. There are only the seconds that seem like hours, minutes that seem like days, days that seem like months, months that seem like years and years that seem like eternity. For three endless hours, in agony, pain and a still and deathly silence, He lived with the "why?"

He entered into the chasm of your pain and suffering and passed through the valley of the shadow of your death because He knew you couldn't go there alone. His rod and His staff were there to comfort you. While He was being crushed, you were being mended. While He was being smitten, you were being healed. While He was being forgotten, you were being remembered. And while He was being abandoned, you were being accepted. That's why. That has always been why. Beyond any shadow of a doubt, that's why!

In a
dark time
the eye
begins to
see.

In a dark time the eye begins to see.

—THEODORE ROETHKE

Chapter 14

Empowered by Your Shadow

Three days later, early on the morning of the feast of first fruits, Mary comes running to tell you and John that she has seen the Master alive. You know that can't be true, for you heard Him say, "It is finished," and breathe His last breath and give up the ghost.

Nevertheless, something in you says you had better just check things out. What do women know anyway? Suddenly, you catch yourself making an unfair assessment of Mary, and you quickly offer a prayer to God requesting His forgiveness for your value judgment and incongruence.

John is trying to keep up with you, but you are just too fast for him. When you get there, you see that the stone is rolled away, and you peek in. Nothing is in there but an empty cocoon that was shaped like a man. You recall unwrapping Lazarus. Boy, it took a long time because he had been well wrapped. But this time the wrappings are still in the shape of a man, but the only thing that is unwrapped is the face cloth. It is as if someone just stepped out of the shell.

You are reminded of a caterpillar that spins itself into a cocoon to sleep. In a moment, its outer shell gives way to its intended destiny. Waking up from the dream of flying, it no longer crawls. It fights its way out of the cocoon and discovers that it now has wings to do what it has always dreamed of doing.

The caterpillar had to pass through the valley of shadows and emerge into its new identity. Those grave clothes, still in the shape of a man, no longer hold Him. He has passed through that valley and has risen above it all! It is too good to be true, so it has to be God!

You get to see Him in the upper room later that night. You are still scared of the high priest, and you know that others have identified you. So you go back to the last place that was safe for you, the place where He washed your feet and promised that you would be able to walk farther.

When you get to the threshold where the water jar had been placed, you cross over it and lock the door behind you. You go over and sit in the seat where you heard Him prophesy your fall and then promise you that you would get up once more to strengthen your brothers. Suddenly there comes a knock at the door, and you think it might be Him. After all, you haven't seen Him. You only saw the grave clothes that had been left behind. Mary said she did see Him, and she said that you should wait for Him in Jerusalem, but that was hours ago. If He really is alive, where is He?

Recognizing Him on the Road of Deep Desire

Actually, He was doing what He loved to do most. He was taking a walk with two of His students. They were on their way back home to a place called "Earnest Longing," or "Deep Desire," which are the exact meanings of the town called Emmaus. This road just so happened to be where He decided to walk that morning.

It was a long walk, and it took Him all day to get there, but He didn't mind. Cleopas and his wife, Mary, were struggling over the Master's death. He stepped into the conversation incognito and began to build a rapport with them. He was such a wise master-teacher. He began carefully and methodically opening up the Scriptures from beginning to end. At the same time He opened up their hearts and minds to experience the Word in a brand-new way so they could understand it for themselves.

Cleopas's and Mary's hearts were on fire. They realized that they had felt this way before, but only around one Man. This Individual didn't look anything like Him, though He sounded a whole lot like Him. By the time they got to their house, they pressed Him to stay with them, even though He intended to go further, or did He?

They persuaded Him to turn in for the evening meal. When they sat down to eat, He reached for the bread, lifted it to heaven, gave thanks and then broke it. At that moment Cleopas looked at his wife, and both their mouths dropped open. They turned to speak to Him, but He had vanished before they could say a word!

They hightailed it back to Jerusalem, running as fast as they could. They huffed and puffed until they arrived at the house with the large upper room. As they climbed the stairs and knocked on the door, your heart stopped. They had knocked at the precise moment that you were wondering why He had not shown Himself alive to you yet.

You go to the door with great anticipation. Yet you are still afraid of the religious crowd who wants to get even with you, so you ask politely who is there. When Cleopas identifies himself, your heart sinks.

You let them in. The ten other disciples had gathered at the room throughout the morning. Thomas, who had been moping somewhere by himself, comes over to listen as the two begin to retell their story of the day's walk home.

The Master Is in Your Midst Once More

Everyone surrounds them as they tell the story. But before they finish, out of nowhere standing right there in the middle of the room as big as life is the Master Himself!

You feel that funny feeling in your feet again, as if you are going to lose your balance. For one of the few times in your life your mouth is open, but you cannot say a thing.

He says to you, "You doubt it's Me. You think you are seeing a ghost again? Ghosts don't have flesh and bones. So, give Me something to eat—that fish over there. Let Me have a bite. Come on; get Me a piece of fish!"

Without another moment's hesitation, you run to the griddle and grab some freshly cooked fish and hand it to Him, and He eats it right in front of your eyes. Whoa! This is a bit much.

Then He reaches over and breathes on you and says, "Receive the breath of God!" When He does that, you feel something go through you that is indescribable and absolutely exquisite. He disappears as quickly as He came. But something inside you is telling you that without a doubt He'll be back!

Going Back to the Past

Days pass. You are getting restless, so you say to James, John and four of the others, "We might as well go fishing: there isn't anything else to do!"

They all follow you—the natural leader that you are—to the Sea of Tiberius. By dusk you have your nets ready and your torches in the boat, and you set out for the open sea. The night passes, and for every throw of the net you catch nothing but seaweed. You hate to admit it, but you are still unable to sort through the pain of your failure and the need to fix your mistakes. You don't feel as though you will ever get the keys to unlock the one door in your heart with the golden lock and unlock the door in the hearts of others where kingdom power can move mountains.

You have wrestled for days, even though you know He is alive and well, even though He told Mary to tell you that God the Father accepts you. God, your Father, loves you. You haven't heard it from Him. You feel as if only He can bring closure to this thing for you. After all, He started the walk of faith in your life. If He began awakening faith in you, it seems logical that only He can bring it to completion.

The night passes, hour by hour, cast by cast, and you catch nothing but seaweed. Late in the midnight hours James claims he can see a shadow of a figure moving back and forth on the beach, but you and John assure him there is nothing there. You are fishing on the most secluded and isolated part of the lake. Besides, no one but the seven of you know your whereabouts, and you're all in the same boat together, aren't you?

A Voice From the Shore

When day breaks and hunger sets in and no fish have been caught, from the beach a figure emerges out of the shadows. You can't quite make out the face, but the voice has a familiar ring to it—at least John thinks so.

"Children, have you caught anything?"

Immediately the hair on the back of your neck bristles. *Who does this guy think he is calling us children; we are grown men!* Somewhere inside you once again, you get this twinge that says, *Simon is still making his presence known!* You decide to answer back, "We have fished all night and haven't caught a thing!"

You had a similar conversation about three and a half years ago with Someone who, at your moment of failure, invited you to try again. When you listened, you caught more fish than you expected and told Him you weren't worthy to be considered someone capable of becoming a master teacher yourself. Nevertheless, He told you not to be afraid, for He would finish what He started in you regardless.

Then you heard this command: "Cast your nets on the other side!"

This also was reminiscent of that moment. Something strange is going on here, but you can't quite figure it out. Your eyes are squinting to see the Man on the shore, and you are positive that He looks nothing like the Master. This is throwing you off. As a matter of fact, every time He has shown up lately to anyone He appears different. He is no longer easily recognizable by His appearance. It has required much more subtle observation to recognize Him. I wonder what His reason is for that—is there any purpose for appearing in a different form?

Casting Your Nets in a New Direction

Without hesitating, John, with his brother's help, hoists the net on the other side, and you grab the net and help, too. The minute the net hits the water the fish actually jump in! That's a new one! When John sees the catch, he knows who the Man is.

He yells, "It's the Lord!"

Normally you take off your clothes when you go swimming. But not this time. You are stripped to the waist, and you put on your overcoat and jump in the water head first, fully dressed, and swim to shore. You look silly all dressed up and soaking wet.

You know it's Him when you get close enough. He looks at you with those eyes, and part of you wants to turn. He already has fish cooking on some hot stones, and you don't even bother to ask where He got them. You do notice that He actually took time to make you breakfast, and your heart is humbled.

While He is serving you the fish, He looks at you and says, "Simon, son of John (you hear Him calling you by your former name, and you accept that you are still that needy person), do you love Me more than these?"

You want to ask, "These what?" You aren't sure whether He's talking about the fish or the other six who are dragging the fish to shore. Somewhat ashamed, knowing He has asked you about unconditional love, you no longer have the ability to offer false pretense. You honestly say, "Lord, I like You. I can't say I love You like that, even though I wish I could. I love You like a brother!"

You are pierced to the heart, just like a hot loaf of bread being pierced in the oven, as He says, "Then feed my lambs!"

"What? I just told You I don't love You unconditionally. The best I can say is I like You!"

"I heard you," He responds. "At least it's honest, and since it's honest and true, I can support you in your longing to get the keys. Feed the young of the flock; take care of the little ones."

"Lord, I blew it. I messed up big time, and I don't need You to give me something to do!"

"Take care of the little ones by feeding them, please!"

While you are chewing a piece of fish that He broiled for you, He asks a second time, "Simon, son of John, do you love Me?"

"This is painful, Lord. No, I don't love You like You are asking; I love You like a brother!"

"Feed my sheep, the ones that are growing up, maturing and learning how to tell the truth. Feed the ones who have moved

beyond knowing they are seen, heard and accepted and are starting to take responsibility for their thoughts and words, their feelings and their behaviors!"

"I am not sure I am capable of doing that, Lord; I am just learning that myself!"

"Great then; that makes you a great choice for feeding them!"
As you eat the last piece of fish on your plate, He waits until you
have half-swallowed and says, "Simon, son of John, do you love
Me like a brother?"

You want to crawl into a hole and die. Now, He is no longer asking you if you love Him unconditionally. He is asking if you at
least love Him the way you say you do, and He wants to know if
you are being real, being transparent, being genuine, being
authentic—being congruent!

This is tough for you because He is demanding total honesty.
You aren't sure you know how it all works. You are Simon, John's
son. You wish you could be Peter, the apostle with the keys, but
you know who you are at this moment.

Half in tears and half in exasperation you say, "I can't hide anything from You. I used to think You didn't see. I used to think I could
mask by behaving in a way to get You to not notice, but I know now
I was just fooling myself. I believe I love You like a brother, and I want
to love You like You love me. Maybe the truth is I like You, even though
I want to love You. This is hard for me, Lord; I am not sure anymore!"

"Govern My people. Be the living stone I called you to be. Pick
up the mantle that fell when you fell, and be the apostle I always
knew you were meant to be. I am giving you the keys; you are
ready for them now!"

"But I don't feel adequate or ready at all. As a matter of fact, I
think You need to pick someone else for this task!"

"No, Peter, you are more ready now than you have ever been
before!"

Forty days ago you wept uncontrollably in the dark on that Friday morning. You have been through a season of transition, and you feel as if you have been through the war. Your fears aren't as intense as they used to be, but they still crop up now and then. Nevertheless, they are manageable. You aren't as quick to make judgments, and you aren't driven as much to take charge of everything, though you still have a take-charge approach to life.

Embracing New Ways

He summons you all together for one last meal, and you know that this is the last time He will gather you this way. He has been appearing to you in various ways during this in-between period because He said He wanted you to get to know Him not by something outward but by something inward, by the Spirit.

You won't "see" Him the way you have been used to seeing Him, but you will "see Him, hear Him and feel Him by the Spirit." It is the dawning of a new day, a new era, and He will be "known" by the Spirit. That is the reason He had to disorient you from every reliance you had on the way you have known Him. From now on you will learn to rely on your inner senses to discern when He is around and moving.

Don't worry; He'll be with you forever. He isn't going to leave you or forsake you. As a matter of fact, in about ten days, something so incredible is going to happen that you are going to experience Him *in you!* That is why you have had to go through the valley of the shadows and face your own death. You have had to die with Him to everything you have known and to bury the shell of your former identity to rise to a new level of awareness. Like the caterpillar that became a butterfly, you are ready to be raised to a whole new life that takes flight.

Taking Flight

He's walking with you again, this time to Bethany, past Martha and Mary's house. Lazarus is waiting outside, and all the followers are going to join you this morning for the walk. You walk past the dead fig tree that isn't even recognizable anymore and up to His favorite spot on the Mount of Olives.

He lifts His hands while you are walking and talking with Him, and all of a sudden you are all enveloped in a cloud, a mist, but it isn't raining.

You can hear voices crying out, "Lift up your heads, O ye gates, and be lifted up, ye everlasting doors, and let the King of Glory come in!"

And somewhere from behind you or in front of you—you can't quite figure out because you have lost all sense of direction in the cloud—another set of voices cries out in song: "Who is this King of Glory?"

The response comes back like an anthem, "The Lord strong and mighty, the Lord mighty in battle. The Lord of Hosts. He is the King of Glory!"[1]

Suddenly the cloud lifts Him above you, and He takes His seat at the right hand of God, high and lifted up just as Isaiah saw Him. He smiles and blesses you.

As He is lifted up above you, He says, "Go into all the world and preach the good news to everyone. Immerse them in the waters that I have immersed you in, and do it in the name of the Father and the Son and the Spirit. Teach them to observe all the things I have commanded you. And don't worry about what words to use, for the right words will flow out of you like a river because My Spirit will give you what to say. Remember, stop looking for Me in the ways you have known Me. You will know Me by My Spirit, and I will be with you always. Now, go wait in Jerusalem until you are clothed with power from on high. And by the way, Peter, don't ask how you will know. Trust Me, you will know when I clothe you!"

Then He is received out of your sight, but not out of your life or your presence.

Becoming Empowered

Ten days later, one hundred twenty of you are in that same upper room, praying and waiting. At about nine in the morning on the Day of Pentecost, when Jews from all over the known world have come to celebrate the wheat harvest, you are all together in agreement. Can you imagine that? You have finally come to agree on more than you disagree on.

You love one another, care for one another and esteem one another as more important than yourselves.

Someone just felt inspired a while ago to read one of David's psalms:

> Behold, how good and how pleasant it is
> For brothers to dwell together in unity![2]

When he gets to the end, something grips your hearts like a vice when these words are uttered:

> For there the Lord commanded the blessing—life forever.[3]

Suddenly there comes from heaven the sound of a mighty rushing wind. It fills the whole house where you are sitting, and there appears on each of your heads fiery tongues with flames every color of the rainbow. You all begin to speak in the languages of those who are visiting from the surrounding nations.

You have no idea how you are doing it, but everyone who hears the noise comes rushing to where you all are, and they hear the Word of God in their native tongue. It is absolutely awesome. You are so caught up that you don't know whether to laugh or cry, so you do both.

The twelve of you are just overwhelmed by what you are all experiencing. The supernatural event spills out into the street. Some people begin to make fun of you because it doesn't make sense. There was a day you might have reacted, but not today. You are different now, and you have the grace not to react.

The crowd becomes so large it takes up the entire street and is still growing. Word spreads that something is going on in the upper room. You are all in the middle of the city, and the crowd is in the multiplied thousands. You don't know what to do.

Some people are asking, "What is going on?

Others are crying out, "Will someone explain this to me? I hear talk about God in a language that I can understand, not like all the rituals in the temple. I feel as if God is drawing close to me. Will someone tell me what this is all about?"

You look at John and James and ask them to say something, and they look at you blankly, not knowing what to say. Then you look at Nathaniel, and he is on the floor talking a mile a minute and is oblivious to what is going on around him. Where is Simon the Zealot? Come on, Simon, say something. But he's at a loss for words. You look at Matthew, and he is busy doing what he has always done. He's writing down his observations. Then you ask Thomas, who says that he eventually will preach some day, but he doubts that his voice is commanding enough to satisfy what the crowd needs at the moment.

At that moment, all eyes are on you. The brothers throw you the ball and tell you to take it and run with it! You are reluctant because you have always been the first to open your mouth. Now, since that journey through the valley of shadows, you are quick to hear and slow to speak.

Your Shadow Heals

Now a voice you have known so well speaks from somewhere within you.

"Behold, I give you the keys of the kingdom of heaven. Whatever you bind on earth, I'll bind in heaven. Whatever you loose on earth, I'll loose in heaven. Go for it! Your name is Peter, and on this rock you and I will kick in the gates of hell!"

For the first time in your new life you take your stand with your brothers. You are not standing alone. You realize that you need them, so you stand in all their strength as well as your own. Something feels as though a door unlocked inside of you. It was the one door that you didn't have the key to unlock, the one with the golden lock—the one that leads to the kingdom within you!

You can hear it unlock, and suddenly the light of the glory of God is released from your innermost being. It is Christ in you, the hope of glory! Your countenance changes; you are covered in the light of a glory that you saw once before on the Mount of Transfiguration.

As you open your mouth to speak, another voice preaches with you and through you. Three thousand people come running out from behind the locked doors of their own prisons and connect with your message!

You are stunned, overwhelmed and exhilarated. You are standing in the light of confidence, clothed in the glory of your true identity. You have passed through the valley of the shadows, and your shadows are no longer blocking your way. They are behind you as a testimony to what you have passed through.

Not many days from now, when you walk by the sick and the diseased, your shadow will fall upon others who need what you now have. The shadow that once prevented you from getting to where you are will heal others—beyond the shadow of doubt!

Notes

Foreword: Dance the Night Away

1. C. S. Lewis, *Mere Christianity* (n.p., 1960), 151–152.
2. Robert G. Tuttle, Jr., *Can We Talk? Sharing Your Faith in a Pre-Christian World* (Nashville: Abingdon, 1999), 20–21.
3. Dov Peretz Elkins, "Hasidic Wisdom for the Heart and Soul," *Sacred Journey* 47 (October 1996), as quoted in *Sacred Journey* 51 (February 2000), 62.
4. With thanks to John M. Buchanan for pointing me to this metaphor in "Steadfast," Fourth Presbyterian Church, 3 December 2000.

Chapter 1: Drowning in an Ocean of Doubt

1. See Proverbs 14:10.
2. See James 1:17.
3. See Isaiah 30:21.

Chapter 2: Finding Healing From the Robbery of the Spirit

1. See John 10:10.

Chapter 3: Dredging Up Hidden Fears

1. Actually, I don't remember my feet touching the ground once he grabbed me by the upper arm—they were certainly moving, yet the earth was far from my two little feet.

2. This is not his real name just in case he reads the book and wants to fight again.
3. See 2 Corinthians 7:5.
4. Salvador Dali, *The Secret Life of Salvador Dali* (New York: Dover, 1993).

CHAPTER 4: CASTING SHADOWS OF INNER CONFLICT

1. See Matthew 10:39.
2. See Psalm 23:4.
3. See Psalm 73, THE MESSAGE.
4. Walter Brueggemann, *Finally Comes the Poet* (Minneapolis, MN: Fortress Press, 1989).
5. Ibid., 15–16.
6. See John 12:24.

CHAPTER 5: STRUCTURES OF INTERNAL BELIEFS

1. See Matthew 21:19.
2. See Roman 8:22.
3. See Matthew 21:21.
4. Moshe Mykoff, *The Empty Chair* (Woodstock, VT: Jewish Lights, 1994), 20.

CHAPTER 6: SABOTAGING STATES OF MIND

1. See Revelation 3:20.
2. See 2 Timothy 1:7, KJV.

CHAPTER 7: BREAKING THE POWER OF AGREEMENTS

1. See Romans 10:17.
2. See 1 Timothy 6:12.
3. See 2 Corinthians 5:17.
4. See Philippians 4:8.

Chapter 8: The Inner Language of Images and Symbols

1. See 1 Corinthians 2:10–14.
2. See Proverbs 20:27.
3. See 1 Corinthians 14:25.
4. See 1 Corinthians 2:11.
5. See Mark 4:11–12.
6. See Matthew 9:36.
7. See John 14:6.
8. See Mark 8:22–26.
9. See Mark 8:24.
10. See Psalm 1:3.

Chapter 9: Now Comes a Stranger

1. See Isaiah 55:12.
2. See Joshua 3:13.
3. See Romans 10:17.
4. See Matthew 11:15.
5. See Revelation 3:7.

Chapter 10: Learning to Walk on Water

1. See 1 John 4:20.

Chapter 11: Keys to the Kingdom Within You

1. See Matthew 16:17.
2. See Matthew 16:18.

Chapter 12: Walls of Resistance

1. See Matthew 7:16.
2. See Psalm 23:4.

3. See Romans 12:2.
4. See Matthew 23:38.
5. See Mark 11:23.
6. See John 12:24.

Chapter 13: Finding Inner Congruence

1. Cyrus the King was promised the hidden treasures of God.
2. See John 13:8.
3. See Zechariah 13:7.
4. See John 14:2.

Chapter 14: Empowered by Your Shadow

1. See Psalm 24:7–10, kjv.
2. See Psalm 133:1.
3. See Psalm 133:3.

You can experience more of *God's grace* & *love!*

If you would like free information on how you can know God more deeply and experience His grace, love and power more fully in your life, simply write or e-mail us. We'll be delighted to send you information that will be a blessing to you.

To check out other titles from **Creation House** that will impact your life, be sure to visit your local Christian bookstore, or call this toll-free number:

1-800-599-5750

For free information from Creation House:

CREATION HOUSE
600 Rinehart Rd.
Lake Mary, FL 32746
www.creationhouse.com